W9-BYK-260

Bruges
DIRECTIONS

WRITTEN AND RESEARCHED BY

Phil Lee

with additional research by

Karoline Densley

ROUGH GUIDES

NEW YORK • LONDON • DELHI
www.roughguides.com

es bieren van 't

Abbaye de Abdij van

Leffe

BELLE-VU
KRIEK

Brugse
Straffe Hendrik

VIEUX TEMP

Hoegaarden
Witbier ~ Bière blanche

Jupiler

Contents

Introduction to

Bruges

In 1896 the novelist and playwright Arnold Bennett complained, "The difference between Bruges and other cities is that in the latter you look about for the picturesque, while in Bruges, assailed on every side by the picturesque, you look curiously for the unpicturesque, and don't find it easily."

Perhaps so, but for the modern palate, battered by postwar development, Bruges' blend of antique architectural styles, from tiny brick cottages to gracious Georgian mansions, is a welcome relief – and retreat. It certainly brings out the romance in many of its visitors – stay here long enough and you can't help but be amazed by the number of couples wandering its canals hand-in-hand, cheek-to-cheek. Neither does it matter much that a fair slice of Bruges is not quite what it seems: many buildings are not the genuine article, but are carefully constructed to resemble their medieval predecessors. Bruges has spent time and

When to visit

Bruges is an **all-year destination**, with most attractions and nearly all its bars and restaurants open in winter and summer alike. The city enjoys a fairly standard temperate climate, with warm, if mild, summers and cold winters, without much snow. The **warmest months** are usually June, July and August (averaging 18°C); the **coldest**, December and January (averaging 2°C), when short daylight hours and weak sunlight can make the weather seem colder (and wetter) than it actually is. **Rain** is always a possibility, even in summer, which actually sees a greater degree of rainfall than autumn or winter. Warm days in April and May, when the light has the clarity of springtime, are especially appealing. In summer, the advantage of the sunnier weather is offset by the excessive number of tourists visiting, especially in July and August. If you're planning a short visit, it's worth noting that almost all of the city's museums are closed on Mondays.

▲ Belgian chocolates

money preserving its image, rendering almost everything that's new in various versions of medieval style, and the result is one of Europe's most beautiful city centres, whose charms are supplemented by a clutch of museums, plus lots of inviting restaurants and bars.

Medieval Bruges prospered as a lynchpin of the cloth trade, turning high-quality English wool into clothing that was exported all over the known world. It was an immensely profitable business and one that made Bruges a focus of international trade. Through the city's harbours, Flemish cloth was exchanged for hogs from Denmark, spices from Venice, hides from Ireland, wax from Russia, gold and silver from Poland and furs from Bulgaria. However, despite (or perhaps because of) this lucrative state of affairs, Bruges was dogged by war.

Its weavers and merchants were dependent on the goodwill of the kings of England for the wool supply, but their feudal overlords, the counts of Flanders and their successors the dukes of Burgundy, were vassals of the rival king of France. Consequently, whenever France and England were at war – which was often – Bruges found itself in a precarious position.

The Habsburgs swallowed Bruges – and Flanders – into their empire towards the end of the fifteenth century and the sour relations between the new rulers and the Bruggelingen (the citizens of Bruges) led to the city's decline. Economically and politically marooned, Bruges simply withered away, its houses deserted, its canals empty and its money spirited away by the departing merchants. Some four centuries later, Georges Rodenbach's novel *Bruges-la-Morte* alerted well-heeled Europeans to the town's aged, quiet charms, and Bruges attracted its first wave of tourists. Many of them – especially the British – settled here and came to play a leading role in preserving the city's architectural heritage and today Bruges is one of the most popular weekend destinations in Europe.

▲ Bruges on ice

Bruges
AT A GLANCE

The Markt

At the centre of Bruges, this handsome cobbled square was long the commercial heart of the city, and is still home to one of the city's most distinctive medieval landmarks, the Belfort, whose distinctive lantern tower pierces the city's skyline.

▲ The Markt

The Burg

The city's second central square, the Burg is flanked by an especially beautiful group of buildings, including the postcard-perfect Gothic Stadhuis and the Heilig Bloed Basiliek, which holds the city's holiest relic, a phial purportedly containing blood washed from the body of Christ.

South of the Markt

The streets south of the Markt are home to several of the city's key sights, from the medieval Onze Lieve Vrouwekerk and St Janshospitaal museum, through to the whitewashed cottages of the Begijnhof and the Minnewater, the so-called "Lake of Love".

The Groeninge Museum

The superb Groeninge Museum boasts one of the world's finest collections of early Flemish paintings, including works by Jan van Eyck, Rogier van der Weyden, Hans Memling and Hieronymus Bosch.

North and east of the Markt

The areas north and east of the centre are home to an especially beguiling collection of handsome

▲ Rozenhoedkaai

streetscapes, with graceful mansions and intimate brick houses draped along a lattice of slender canals, crisscrossed by dinky little stone bridges.

Damme

A popular day-trip from Bruges, the pretty little village of Damme perches beside a canal 7km to the northeast of the city.

▼ Krinkeldijk, Damme

▲ Guild houses, Graslei, Ghent

Ghent

Ghent's ancient centre holds a glorious set of Gothic buildings, including the stirring St Baafskathedraal (also home to the remarkable *Adoration of the Mystic Lamb* by Jan van Eyck), St Niklaaskerk, the medieval guild houses of the Graslei, and a forbidding castle, Het Gravensteen.

▲ *In den Wittenkop* restaurant

Ideas

The big six sights

Bruges isn't a city of major sights: its real pleasures lie in its charming mix of antique buildings set against a skein of canals, all best absorbed by easy wanderings. Nevertheless, there are a number of attractions you shouldn't leave town without seeing, ranging from the landmark **Belfort** (belfry), overlooking the Markt through to the medieval paintings in the **Groeninge Museum**.

▲ The Belfort

One of the city's most distinctive landmarks, the soaring lantern tower of the Belfort pierces the skyline of central Bruges.

P.53 ▶ THE MARKT

▲ Heilig Bloed Basiliek

The city's most important shrine, home to the revered Holy Blood relic, reputedly washed from the body of the crucified Christ.

P.59 ▶ THE BURG

▼ Begijnhof

Extraordinarily picturesque huddle of white-washed houses which was once home to a self-contained community of unmarried women.

P.77 ▶ SOUTH OF THE MARKT

▼ Sint Janshospitaal

This former hospital is now a museum with a wonderful sample of the paintings of Hans Memling.

P.73 ▶ SOUTH OF THE MARKT

▲ Groeninge Museum

The city's leading museum, internationally famous for its collection of early Flemish paintings.

P.85 ▶ THE GROENINGE MUSEUM

▼ Onze Lieve Vrouwekerk

Topped by one of the tallest spires in Belgium, the rambling Onze Lieve Vrouwekerk is the pick of the city's medieval churches.

P.70 ▶ SOUTH OF THE MARKT

Canalside Bruges

Bruges is famous for its canals, a series of narrow waterways which lattice the city centre and provide a beautiful contrast with its antique buildings. Ornamental today, they were once the city's economic lifeline, with ships sailing into the city from the North Sea via the canal that ran from Damme. There are boat tours of the central canals, but the prettiest stretches can often only be reached on foot.

▲ Gouden Handrei

Home to an eye-catching medley of the canalside outhouses which stand at the end of many city gardens.

P.96 ▶ NORTH AND EAST OF THE MARKT

▲ Minnewater

The "Lake of Love" attracts canoodlers by the score.

P.77 ▶ SOUTH OF THE MARKT

◀ St Bonifaciusbrug

No question, this is the quaintest bridge in Bruges – even if it was built in 1910.

P.68 ▶ SOUTH OF THE MARKT

▶ Rozenhoedkaai

This slender quay provides an exquisite view of the Belfort.

P.67 ▶ SOUTH OF THE MARKT

▼ Augustijnenbrug

The city's oldest bridge, named after the Augustinian monks who once lived nearby.

P.96 ▶ NORTH AND EAST OF THE MARKT

▲ Jan van Eyckplein

Once a centre of merchant life, this quiet square overlooks the Spiegelrei canal.

P.96 ▶ NORTH AND EAST OF THE MARKT

Medieval Flemish art

Throughout the medieval period, Flanders was one of the most artistically productive parts of Europe, with all the Flemish cloth towns – and especially Bruges and Ghent – trying to outdo one another with the quality of their **religious art**. Today, the works of these early Flemish painters are highly prized, and there's an excellent selection on display in Bruges, most memorably at the **Groeninge Museum** and in **St Janshospitaal**.

▲ Jan Provoost

Provoost packed a real punch into his paintings, as here, showing a miser attempting to bargain with death.

P.89 ▸ THE GROENINGE MUSEUM

▲ Hieronymus Bosch

Bosch's religious allegories are filled with macabre visions of tortured people and grotesque beasts.

P.89 ▸ THE GROENINGE MUSEUM

▼ Jan van Eyck

Arguably the greatest of the early Flemish masters, van Eyck was a key figure in the development of oil painting, modulating its tones to create paintings of extraordinary clarity and realism.

P.85 ▸ THE GROENINGE MUSEUM

▲ Rogier van der Weyden

Weyden's serene portraits of religious scenes and local bigwigs were much admired across western Europe.

P.86 ▸THE GROENINGE MUSEUM

▼ Gerard David

Typical of the work of David, this triptych is a restrained meditation on the baptism of Christ.

P.88 ▸ THE GROENINGE MUSEUM

Modern Belgian art

René Magritte, one of Surrealism's leading lights, was Belgian, and his work exemplifies the enduring Belgian penchant for the bizarre and macabre which can be traced back to the grotesques of James Ensor, and even Hieronymus Bosch. Similarly appealing to Belgian sensibilities was Expressionism, whose exaggerated shapes and colours are evident in the eye-catching canvases of Constant Permeke, a member of the Expressionist group of painters who took up residence outside Ghent in the early twentieth century.

▲ Paul Delvaux

Delvaux adopted his own salacious "What-the-butler-saw" interpretation of the Surrealist movement.

P.92 ▶ THE GROENINGE MUSEUM

▲ René Magritte

Magritte used ordinary images in a dream-like way, with strange, disconcerting juxta-positions.

P.92 ▶ THE GROENINGE MUSEUM

▼ James Ensor

Ensor painted and drew macabre, disturbing works – often of skulls and skeletons – whose haunted style prefigured Expressionism.

P.92 ▶ THE GROENINGE MUSEUM

▼ Fernand Khnopff

Khnopff was Belgium's leading Symbolist, his unsettling canvases playing with notions of lust and desire.

P.91 ▶ THE GROENINGE MUSEUM

▲ Constant Permeke

Belgium's leading Expressionist, whose bold, deeply shaded canvases can be found in many Belgian galleries.

P.91 ▶ THE GROENINGE MUSEUM

▲ Jean Delville

Expressionist who set about his religious preoccupations with gigantic gusto.

P.91 ▶ THE GROENINGE MUSEUM

Churches

Profoundly Catholic for most of its history, Bruges possesses a liberal sprinkling of churches. The finest are Gothic, built on the profits of the cloth trade and dating back to the thirteenth century, though these were all modified in later centuries – a tower here and an aisle there. The second major period of church-building in Bruges was in the nineteenth century, when the neo-Gothic style ruled the architectural roost.

▲ Jeruzalemkerk

The most unusual church in Bruges surmounted by an idiosyncratic lantern tower.

P.99 ▶ NORTH AND EAST OF THE MARKT

▲ St Jakobskerk

Sturdy Gothic church distinguished by the fancy burial chapel of Ferry de Gros.

P.93 ▶ NORTH AND EAST OF THE MARKT

▼ St Walburgakerk

Handsome Baroque church built for the Jesuits in the seventeenth century.

P.98 ▶ NORTH AND EAST OF THE MARKT

▲ St Annakerk

A modest and largely modern parish church with slender architectural lines and an ornate rood screen.

P.98 ▶ NORTH AND EAST OF THE MARKT

▶ St Salvatorskathedraal

A sterling Gothic edifice with a spectacular tower and an interior stuffed with all sorts of ecclesiastical bric-a-brac.

P.74 ▶ SOUTH OF THE MARKT

▼ Onze Lieve Vrouwekerk

This intriguing medieval church is home to a Michelango Madonna in the nave and medieval paintings in the choir.

P.70 ▶ SOUTH OF THE MARKT

Museums

Bruges' most important museums are the Groeninge (see p.85) and Sint Janshospitaal (see p.73), home to outstanding collections of **fine art**, and there are more old Flemish paintings in the intriguing Onze-Lieve-Vrouw ter Potterie museum. Bruges was once famous for its **tapestries** and there's a first-rate sample of them in the Gruuthuse, whilst **lace** – another Bruges speciality – is featured in the Kantcentrum (Lace Centre).

▲ Volkskunde Museum

The Volkskunde (Folklore) Museum's string of recreated period rooms, shops and work-shops give the flavour of nineteenth-century Bruges.

P.100 ▶ NORTH AND EAST OF THE MARKT

▲ Arentshuis

Home to a fine selection of the painting and drawings by Bruges-born artist Frank Brangwyn.

P.67 ▶ SOUTH OF THE MARKT

▼ Kantcentrum

The Kantcentrum (Lace Centre) hosts informal demonstrations of traditional lace-making.

P.98 ▶ NORTH AND EAST OF THE MARKT

▲ Gruuthuse

The Gruuthuse holds an outstanding collection of fine and applied art, including a famous bust of Charles V.

P.69 ▶ SOUTH OF THE MARKT

▶ Onze-Lieve-Vrouw ter Potterie

This unusual museum, in a one-time medieval hospital, includes a handsome chapel with lovely stained-glass windows.

P.103 ▶ NORTH AND EAST OF THE MARKT

◀ Archeological Museum

Small museum with an entertaining section on the city's tanners.

P.74 ▶ SOUTH OF THE MARKT

Ghent

Ghent is a larger, more sprawling and less immediately picturesque city than Bruges, but like its neighbour it possesses a stunning cluster of **Gothic buildings** and many delightful, intimate **streetscapes**, with antique brick houses woven around a web of narrow canals. Ghent also lays claim to an excellent **nightlife and restaurant scene**, not to mention what many regard as the world's **greatest painting**, Jan van Eyck's extraordinary *Adoration of the Mystic Lamb*.

▲ Adoration of the Mystic Lamb

Displayed in Ghent's St Baafskathedraal, Jan van Eyck's visionary painting celebrates the Lamb of God, the symbol of Christ's sacrifice.

P.115 ▸ GHENT

▲ S.M.A.K.

The Museum for Contemporary Art features temporary exhibitions of international standard.

P.129 ▸ GHENT

▼ Het Gravensteen

Long the home of the counts of Flanders, Ghent's castle is an intimidating stronghold.

P.123 ▶ GHENT

▲ St Baafskathedraal

At the heart of Ghent, the St Baafskathedraal is one of Belgium's finest Gothic churches.

P.114 ▶ GHENT

▶ St Niklaaskerk

An exquisite example of early Gothic architecture, the angular lines of St Niklaaskerk rise high above central Ghent.

P.119 ▶ GHENT

▼ The Graslei guild houses

The guilds of medieval Ghent were a power to be reckoned with and these were their headquarters.

P.121 ▶ GHENT

Canalside hotels

Some of the classiest hotels in Bruges occupy charming canalside locations, offering delightful views from many of their guest and public rooms. The majority of these hotels occupy grand Neoclassical mansions, but some are in older brick buildings dating back to medieval times.

HOTEL

▲ Die Swaene

Romantic, family-owned hotel in a delightful setting and with luxurious antique furnishings.

P.146 ▸ ACCOMMODATION

▼ Relais Oud Huis Amsterdam

Classic eighteenth-century mansion sympa-
thetically converted into a four-star hotel.

P.147 ▶ ACCOMMODATION

▲ De Tuilerieën

Ornately refurbished eighteenth-century
mansion near the Markt.

P.147 ▶ ACCOMMODATION

▷ Adornes

Excellent hotel in a handsome setting and
with a sleek, modern interior.

P.143 ▶ ACCOMMODATION

▼ Boatel

This former canal barge has been turned
into one of Ghent's most appealing hotels.

P.150 ▶ ACCOMMODATION

Historic hotels

Bruges has a hatful of historic hotels. Some occupy grand nineteenth-century **mansions**; others occupy antique **brick houses;** while others are set in former **monasteries and convents.** All provide extremely comfortable lodgings in a style that matches the historic quality of Bruges itself.

▲ Jacobs

Appealing and reasonably priced hotel in a pleasingly modernized old brick building.

P.148 ▸ ACCOMMODATION

▶ Monasterium Poortackere

The most unusual hotel in Ghent, set in a tidily converted nineteenth-century monastery.

P.150 ▶ ACCOMMODATION

▲ Walburg

Well-appointed hotel in a handsome nineteenth-century mansion.

P.147 ▶ ACCOMMODATION

▼ De Goezeput

Occupying a former convent, this outstanding hotel is one of the best bargains in town.

P.148 ▶ ACCOMMODATION

Hostels

Bruges is well equipped with **hostels**, including an official HI hostel tucked away on the outskirts of town plus several privately run hostels in the centre. All offer inexpensive – if rather spartan – accommodation, either in double rooms or in dormitory beds, and the best also have lively bars and a youthful, friendly atmosphere, making them good places to meet other travellers.

▲ Passage

Arguably the most comfortable and atmospheric hostel in Bruges – and excellent value too.

P.149 ▶ ACCOMMODATION

▲ Charlie Rockets

A handy setting near the Markt and a boisterous crew make this a popular hostel.

P.149 ▸ ACCOMMODATION

▶ Bauhaus

Well-established hostel with a laid-back
atmosphere and some of the cheapest
rooms in the city.

P.149 ▸ ACCOMMODATION

▼ Snuffel Inn

Recently revamped and redecorated by art
students, this is one of the city's friendliest
hostels.

P.149 ▸ ACCOMMODATION

Flemish food

Flemish food is characteristically straightforward and hearty. Pork, beef, game, fish and seafood, especially mussels, herring and eels, remain the staple items, often cooked with butter, cream and herbs, or sometimes beer. **Soup** is also common, hearty stew-like affairs offered in a huge tureen from which you can help yourself – a satisfying and reasonably priced meal in itself.

▲ Mussels and chips

Belgium's unofficial national dish, you won't go far in Bruges without seeing great heaps of mussels (*mosselen*) served up in giant tureens.

▶ Waterzooi

A delicious and filling soup-cum-stew, served either with either chicken (*van kip*) or fish (*van riviervis*).

◀ Haring

The Flemings love their herring – preferably (raw) fillets with onions in a bread roll.

▶ Karbonaden

Cubes of beef marinated in beer and cooked with herbs and onions – a delicious combination.

◀ Paling in't Groen

Traditional Flemish dish consisting of eel braised in a green – usually spinach – sauce with herbs.

Restaurants

Bruges boasts a huge number of **restaurants**, ranging from deluxe establishments where you can sample exquisite Flemish and French cuisine, through to rudimentary, tourist-orientated places serving up filling meals at bargain-basement prices. Mercifully, very few are owned by chains and consequently the vast majority are small and cosy, with the chef – or chef-owner – hovering around to make sure everything is up to scratch.

▲ **Den Dyver**

Formal, long-established restaurant specializing in Flemish dishes cooked in beer.

P.81 ▶ SOUTH OF THE MARKT

▲ **Het Dagelijks Brood**

Smashing little café-cum-restaurant with a fine line in breads and soups.

P.64 ▶ THE BURG

▼ Spinola

A handsome setting and delicious food make this one of the city's most recommendable restaurants.

P.105 ▸ NORTH AND EAST OF THE MARKT

▲ De Lotteburg

This smart establishment is probably the best seafood restaurant in town.

P.82 ▸ SOUTH OF THE MARKT

▼ Cafedraal

Chic restaurant offering a wide range of French and Flemish dishes.

P.80 ▸ SOUTH OF THE MARKT

Belgian beer

There are about 700 Belgian beers to choose from, and the range is simply mind-boggling: there are red beers and brown beers, fruit beers and wheat beers, not to mention super-strong Trappist beers and tart Lambic beers fermented with wild yeast. Most bars in Bruges have a beer menu and, although it's unlikely that any one establishment will have all those listed here, most should have at least a couple.

▲ Kwak

This sweet amber ale is served in distinctive hourglasses placed in a wooden stand.

▶ Geuze
Double-fermented beer with a tart flavour and yellow colour.

◀ Orval
Strong, amber ale produced in an abbey in the south of Belgium.

▼ Kriek
Delightfully refreshing brew flavoured with cherries.

▲ Chimay
tried

World-famous brew made by Trappist monks. Try the red top (7%) or the leg-liquefying blue (9%).

liked

Bars

Few would say Bruges' **bars** are cutting-edge, but neither are they staid and dull and, if you know where to go, drinking in the city can be a delight. The city's bars run the gamut from traditional, neighbourhood haunts to sleek modern places and the Euro-style pavement cafés which flank the Markt.

▲ Het Dreupelhuisje

Jenever (Dutch gin) enthusiasts should make straight for this intimate little bar.

P.83 ▸ SOUTH OF THE MARKT

▼ Oud Vlissinghe

Eccentric old bar with oodles of wood panelling, long wooden tables and a pleasant beer garden.

P.106 ▶ NORTH AND EAST OF THE MARKT

▼ Wijnbar Est

The decor may be uninspiring, but the wine list is the best in the city.

P.84 ▶ SOUTH OF THE MARKT

▲ De Garre

With an enterprising beer menu and jazzy background music, this is one of the city's most enjoyable bars.

P.58 ▶ THE MARKT

▼ De Republiek

Fashionably cool and youthful bar with a substantial beer menu.

P.106 ▶ NORTH AND EAST OF THE MARKT

Shopping: food and drink

With so much space dedicated to tourism, regular **shopping for food and drink** plays second fiddle in central Bruges, but there are a string of places devoted to Belgium's gastronomic holiest of holy – **beer and chocolate**. With chocolate, it's worth remembering that you really do pay for what you get: the cheaper the product, the more likely it is to have a greater percentage of sugar.

▲ Deldycke

The best delicatessen in town, perfect for preparing a picnic.

P.56 ▶ THE MARKT

▼ Chocolate Line

Most chocolate shops in Bruges are chains, but this one isn't – and the chocolates are all the better for it.

P.78 ▶ SOUTH OF THE MARKT

▲ Jenever

The Belgians have a penchant for *jenever* (Dutch gin); the Bottleshop (see below) has a wide variety.

P.56 ▶ THE MARKT

▶ The Bottle Shop

There are several hundred different types of Belgian beer and this cheerful shop stocks most of them.

P.56 ▶ THE MARKT

◀ La Pasta

Italian specialist stocking every type of pasta and Italian wine you can think of.

P.57 ▶ THE MARKT

Shopping: clothes and fashion

When it comes to clothes and fashion, Bruges is a minor league player, but it does have a handful of **designer shops** where you can pick up some great and very varied gear: Belgium has a lively fashion scene, and its leading designers – like Olivier Strelli – have an international reputation.

▲ Knapp Targa

Arguably the best clothes shop in town, with a wide range of chic clothes, from classic labels to more adventurous styles.

P.79 ▶ SOUTH OF THE MARKT

▼ Quicke

The best shoe shop in town, showcasing top European designers.

P.80 ▶ SOUTH OF THE MARKT

▲ Olivier Strelli

Belgium's most famous clothes designer, known for his simple but modern and elegantly tailored designs for both men and women.

P.57 ▶ THE MARKT

▼ Rex Spirou

Adventurous designer fashions for the under-30s, plus plenty of accessories.

P.57 ▶ THE MARKT

Speciality shops

Bruges is a well-heeled city and its prosperity is reflected in its **speciality shops**, selling everything from high-spec furnishings and fittings through to wallet-emptying antiques and locally made lace.

▲ Kasimirs

Antiques are big business in Bruges, and this immaculate place makes for excellent browsing.

P.78 ▸ SOUTH OF THE MARKT

▼ Callebert

The Belgians are strong on contemporary, domestic design – everything from kettles to sofas – and Callebert proves the point.

P.56 ▸ THE MARKT

▲ TinTin Shop

Belgium's bequiffed cartoon hero has spawned a cottage industry of keepsakes and souvenirs.

P.58 ▸ THE MARKT

▼ Bilbo

The pick of Bruges' record shops, both for new and old CDs and vinyl.

P.78 ▸ SOUTH OF THE MARKT

Festivals

Bruges puts on an ambitious programme of **festivals** and **special events**. One or two, like the solemn Heilig Bloedprocessie, are deeply embedded in the city's history, while others are geared up for the inhabitants of the small surrounding villages. The majority, however – especially the **performing arts** and **film festivals** – are primarily aimed at the city's many visitors.

▲ Gentse Feesten

Ten-day party in Ghent with bands and buskers, an outdoor market, plus lashings of alcohol.

P.159 ▶ ESSENTIALS

▶ Heilig Bloedprocessie

Held on Ascension Day, the Procession of the
Holy Blood celebrates Bruges' holiest icon, a
phial holding drops of Christ's blood.

P.159 ▸ ESSENTIALS

▼ Meifoor

Locals warm up at this annual fun-fair, held
from mid-April to mid-May.

P.158 ▸ ESSENTIALS

▼ Kerstmarkt

Bruges' Christmas market is a picturesque
affair with open-air stalls and a skating rink.

P.160 ▸ ESSENTIALS

Musical Bruges

Bruges may be a small city, but musically it more than pulls its weight with an outstanding programme of live classical concerts plus rock, jazz and world music. Neighbouring Ghent and Ostend chip in with their musical contributions, too. Many of Bruges' prime performances are at the Concertgebouw, the brand new concert hall on 't Zand, where the acoustics are first-rate.

▲ Festival van Vlaanderen

Long-established festival featuring classical music concerts in historic locations.

P.159 ▶ ESSENTIALS

▲ Musica Antiqua

Medieval music at its most inventive, performed over two weeks in late July and early August.

P.159 ▸ ESSENTIALS

▶ Cactusfestival

Three-day rap, roots and R&B knees-up held over the second weekend of July.

P.159 ▸ ESSENTIALS

▼ Concertgebouw

Bruges' premier concert hall, opened in 2002 and boasting outstanding acoustics.

P.158 ▸ ESSENTIALS

Places

The Markt

Passing through Bruges in 1820, William Wordsworth declared that this was where he discovered "a deeper peace than in deserts found". He was neither the first nor the last Victorian to fall in love with the place and by the 1840s there was a substantial British colony here, its members captured and enraptured by the city's medieval architecture and air of lost splendour. Civil service and army pensions went much further in Bruges than back home and the expatriates were not slow to exercise their economic muscle, applying an architectural Gothic Revival brush to parts of the city that weren't "medieval" enough. Time and again, they intervened in municipal planning decisions, allying themselves to likeminded Flemings in a movement which changed, or at least modified, the face of the city – and ultimately paid out megabucks with the arrival of mass tourism in the 1960s.

Thus, Bruges is not the perfectly preserved medieval city described by much tourist literature, but rather a clever, frequently seamless combination of medieval original and nineteenth- and sometimes twentieth-century additions. This is especially true of the city centre and its principal

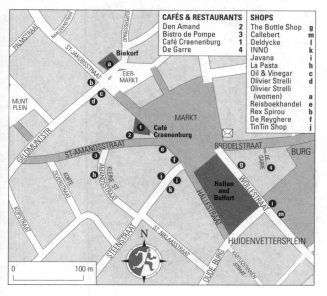

CAFÉS & RESTAURANTS	
Den Amand	2
Bistro de Pompe	3
Café Craenenburg	1
De Garre	4

SHOPS	
The Bottle Shop	g
Callebert	m
Deldycke	l
INNO	k
Javana	i
La Pasta	h
Oil & Vinegar	c
Olivier Strelli	d
Olivier Strelli (women)	a
Reisboekhandel	e
Rex Spirou	b
De Reyghere	f
TinTin Shop	j

PLACES

The Markt

You can buy a **combined ticket** (€15) for any five of Bruges' fourteen municipal museums – including the Stadhuis, Belfort, Groeninge, Gruuthuse and Memling. The ticket is available at any of the museums, and from the tourist office. Note that all these museums are closed on Mondays.

square, the Markt, an airy open space overlooked by the mighty Belfort and flanked on its other three sides by rows of gabled buildings, with horse-drawn buggies clattering over the cobbles between. The biscuit-tin buildings flanking the square form a charming ensemble, largely mellow ruddy-brown brick, each gable compatible with but slightly different from its neighbour. Most are late nineteenth- or twentieth-century recreations – or reinventions – of older

buildings, though the Post Office, which hogs the east side of the square, is a thunderous neo-Gothic edifice which refuses to camouflage its more modern construction.

The Monument to Pieter de Coninck and Jan Breydel

The burghers of nineteenth-century Bruges were keen to put something suitably civic in the middle of the Markt and the result is the conspicuous monument to Pieter de Coninck, of the guild of weavers, and Jan Breydel, dean of the guild of butchers. Standing close together, they clutch the hilt of the same sword, their faces turned to the south in slightly absurd poses of heroic determination – and a far cry from the gory events which first made them local heroes. At dawn on Friday, May 18, 1302, in what was later called the Bruges Matins, their force of rebellious Flemings crept into the city

▲ THE MARKT

▲ BREYDAL AND CONINCK MONUMENT

The Café Craenenburg

Occupying a relatively undistinguished modern building on the corner of St Amandsstraat, the Craenenburg Café marks the site of the eponymous medieval mansion in which the guildsmen of Bruges imprisoned the Habsburg heir, Archduke Maximilian, for three months in 1488 in retaliation for the archduke's efforts to limit the city's privileges. Maximilian made all sorts of promises to escape their clutches, but a few weeks after his release his father, Emperor Frederick III, turned up with an army to take imperial revenge, with a bit of hanging here and a bit of burning there. Maximilian became emperor in 1493 and never forgave Bruges, not only failing to honour his promises but also doing his considerable best to push trade north to its great rival, Antwerp.

and massacred the unsuspecting French garrison, putting to the sword anyone who couldn't correctly pronounce the Flemish shibboleth *schild en vriend* ("shield and friend"). Later the same year, the two guildsmen went on to lead the city's contingent in the Flemish army that defeated the French at the Battle of the Golden Spurs – no surprise, then, that the monument takes its cue from the battle rather than the massacre. Interestingly enough, the statue was actually unveiled twice. In July 1887 a local committee pulled back the drapes to celebrate Coninck and Breydel as Flemings, whilst in August the city council organized an official opening, when King Leopold II honoured them as Belgians.

The Belfort

Tues–Sun 9.30am–5pm, last entry 4.15pm; €5. Filling out the south side of the Markt, but entered via the Hallen, the domineering Belfort (belfry) is a potent symbol of civic pride and municipal independence, its distinctive octagonal lantern visible for miles across the surrounding polders. The Belfort was begun in the thirteenth

A Bruges timeline

865 Bruges founded as a coastal stronghold against the Vikings by Baldwin Iron Arm, first count of Flanders.

Tenth century The beginnings of the wool industry in Flanders. The leading Flemish cloth towns are Bruges and Ghent.

Twelfth to late fourteenth century The Flemish cloth industry becomes dependent on English wool. Flanders enjoys an unprecedented economic boom and its merchants become immensely rich. Increasing tension – and bouts of warfare – between the merchants and weavers of Flanders and their feudal overlords, the counts of Flanders and the kings of France.

1384 The dukes of Burgundy inherit Flanders.

1419 Philip the Good, Duke of Burgundy, makes Bruges his capital. The Burgundian court becomes known across Europe for its cultured opulence. Philip dies in 1467.

1482 Mary, the last of the Burgundians, dies and her territories – including Flanders – revert to her husband, Maximilian, a Habsburg prince. Thus, Flanders is absorbed into the Habsburg empire.

1490s onwards Decline of the Flemish cloth industry.

1530s Bruges' international trade collapses and the town slips into a long decline.

Mid-sixteenth to seventeenth century The Protestants of modern-day Belgium and The Netherlands rebel against their Catholic Habsburg kings. A long and cruel series of wars ensues. Eventually, The Netherlands win their independence – as the United Provinces – and the south, including Flanders, is reconstituted as the Spanish Netherlands.

1700 The last of the Spanish Habsburgs, King Charles II, dies; the War of the Spanish Succession follows.

1713 The Treaty of Utrecht passes what is now Belgium to the Austrians – as the Austrian Netherlands.

1794 Napoleon occupies the Austrian Netherlands and annexes it to France the following year.

1815 Napoleon is defeated at Waterloo and the Austrian Netherlands becomes half of the newly constiuted Kingdom of The Netherlands.

1830 A rebellion leads to the collapse of the new kingdom and the creation of an independent Belgium, including Flanders.

Mid- to late nineteenth century Much of Belgium industrializes, but not Bruges, whose antique charms attract a first wave of tourists.

century, when the town was at its richest and most extravagant, but has had a blighted history. The original wooden version was struck by lightning and burned to the ground in 1280. The present brick replacement, with blind arcading, turrets and towers, was constructed in its place, receiving its octagonal stone lantern and a second wooden spire in the 1480s, though the new spire was lost to a thunderstorm a few years

later. Undeterred, the Flemings promptly added a third spire, though when this went up in smoke in 1741 the locals gave up, settling for the present structure with the addition of a stone parapet in 1822. It's a pity they didn't have another go, if only to sabotage Longfellow's metre in his dire but oft-quoted poem "The Belfry of Bruges": "In the market place of Bruges/Stands the Belfry old and brown/

▲ THE BELFORT

Thrice consumed and thrice rebuilt ...", and so on. Few would say the Belfort is good-looking – it's large and really rather clumsy – but it does have a certain ungainly charm, though this was lost on G.K. Chesterton, who described it as "an unnaturally long-necked animal, like a giraffe".

The Hallen

Entry to the Belfort is via the quadrangular Hallen at its base. Now used for temporary exhibitions, the Hallen is a much-restored edifice dating from the thirteenth century and modelled on the Lakenhalle (Cloth Hall) at Ieper. In the middle, overlooked by a long line of galleries, is a rectangular courtyard, which originally served as the town's principal market, its cobblestones once crammed with merchants and their wares. On the north side of the courtyard, up a flight of steps, is the belfry entrance.

Inside, the belfry staircase begins innocuously, but gets steeper and very much narrower nearer the top. On the way up, it passes several chambers, beginning with the Treasury Room, where the town charters

and money chest were locked for safekeeping behind a set of fancy – and still surprisingly well-preserved – iron grilles. Here also is an iron trumpet with which a watchman could warn the town of a fire outbreak – though given the size of the trumpet, it's hard to believe this was very effective.

The Carillon Chamber

Carrying on up the staircase, you soon reach the Carillon Chamber, where you can observe the slow turning of the large spiked drum that controls the 47 bells of the municipal carillon. The largest bell weighs no less than six tonnes. Like other Flemish cities, bells were first used in Bruges in the fourteenth century as a means

▲ THE CARILLON CHAMBER

Carillon Concerts, which are audible all over the city centre, are performed from late June to September on Monday, Wednesday and Saturday (9–10pm) and Sunday (2.15–3pm), and from October to mid-June (Wed, Sat & Sun 2.15–3pm).

of regulating the working day, and as such reflected the development of a wage economy – employers were keen to keep tabs on their employees. Bells also served as a sort of public address system with everyone understanding the signals: pealing bells, for example, announced good news; tolling bells summoned the city to the Markt; and a rapid sequence of bells warned of danger. By the early fifteenth century a short peal of bells marked the hour, and from this developed the carillon (*beiaard*), with Bruges installing its present version in the middle of the eighteenth century. The city still employs a full-time bell-ringer and you're likely to see him fiddling around preparing his concerts in the Carillon Room, a small and intimate little cubby hole right near the top of the belfry. A few stairs up from here you emerge onto the roof of the Belfort, which offers fabulous views over the city, especially in the late afternoon, when the warm colours of the town are at their deepest.

Shops

The Bottle Shop
Wollestraat 13 ☎050/34 99 80. Daily 10am–7pm, closed second week in Jan. Just off the Markt – so very popular with tourists – this bright and cheerful establishment stocks several hundred types of beer, oodles of whisky and *jenever* (gin), as well as all sorts of special glasses to drink them from – the Belgians have specific glasses for many of their beers.

Callebert
Wollestraat 25 ☎050/33 50 61, ⓦ www.callebert.be. Tues–Sat 10am–noon & 2–6pm. Sun 2–6pm. Bruges' top contemporary homeware, ceramics and furniture store, featuring leading brands such as Alessi and Bodum, as well as less familiar names. They also stock everything from bags, watches and jewellery to household utensils, textiles and tableware, while the shop's art gallery presents the best of contemporary design, primarily in glass and ceramics, along with calligraphy and photography.

Deldycke
Wollestraat 23 ☎050/33 43 35. Daily except Tues 9.30am–6pm. The best delicatessen in town, with helpful service and every treat you can think of – from snails and on up the evolutionary tree – plus pâtés and a good selection of beer.

INNO
Steenstraat 11–15 ☎050/33 06 03. Mon–Sat 9.15am–6pm. The best department store in town, spread over four floors and selling everything from high-quality clothes and perfumes through to leather goods, underwear, household utensils and jewellery. If you don't find what you're looking for here, try HEMA, nearby at Steenstraat 73 (Mon–Sat 9am–6pm).

Javana
Steenstraat 6 ☎050/33 36 05, ⓦ www.javana.be. Mon–Sat 9am–6.30pm. Javana has been selling the best coffees and teas in the world from these neat little

premises for over fifty years, and also stocks the full range of accessories for coffee- and tea-making.

La Pasta

Kleine Sint Amandsstraat 12 ☎050/34 23 01. Tues–Fri 9.30am–1pm & 2–6pm, Sat 9.30am–6pm. Popular with locals, this cosy, family-run food shop sells everything Italian, its speciality being delicious ready-cooked meals. Also stocks a good range of Italian and French wines.

Oil & Vinegar

Geldmuntstraat 11 ☎050/34 56 50, ⓦwww.oilvinegar.com. Mon–Sat 10am–6pm. Mediterranean gift-shop-cum-food store offering an assortment of sauces, mustards and cooking oils in attractive jars and glass bottles, plus a good range of Tuscan cookbooks.

Olivier Strelli (for men)

Geldmuntstraat 19 ☎050/33 26 75, ⓦwww.strelli.be. Mon–Sat 10am–12.30pm & 1.30–6.30pm. Men's branch of Belgium's well-known designer selling pricey contemporary tailored designs with a touch of individuality; the fitted shirts and soft woollens with characteristic diagonal zips are particularly popular.

Olivier Strelli (for women)

Eiermarkt 3☎050/34 38 37, ⓦwww.strelli.be. Mon–Sat 10am–6.30pm. One of Belgium's most established designers, Strelli has been creating simple but modern clothes for years.

His designs include tailored trousers and fitted jackets, often in muted tones with the odd splash of colour thrown in. Pricey.

Reisboekhandel

Markt 13 ☎050/49 12 29, ⓦwww.reisboekhandel.be. Mon–Sat 9.30am–12.30pm & 1.30–6pm. Travel specialist branch of De Reyghere (see below), with a wide selection of travel guides, some in English, plus road and city maps and hiking and cycling maps of the surrounding areas. Also stocks travel-related English–language magazines.

Rex Spirou

Geldmuntstraat 18 ☎050/34 66 50. Mon–Fri 9.30am–6.30pm, Sat 9.30am–7pm. Chic and sharp designer clothes for the young and cool – or at least the self-conscious – plus a good line in accessories, from jewellery to bags and belts. Pricey.

De Reyghere

Markt 12 ☎050/33 34 03. Mon–Sat 8.30am–6.15pm. Founded over one hundred years ago, De Reyghere is something of a local institution and a meeting

▲ CAFÉ CRAENENBURG

place for every book-lover in town. The shop stocks a good range of domestic and foreign literature, art and gardening books and travel guides, and is also good for international newspapers, magazines and periodicals.

TinTin Shop

Steenstraat 3 ☎ 050/33 42 92, ⓦ www.tintinshopbrugge.be. April–Sept Mon–Sat 9.30am–6pm, Sun 11am–6pm; Oct–March closed Wed. Souvenir-cum-comic shop cashing in on on Hergé's quiffed hero, with all sorts of Tintin tackle from T-shirts to comics.

Cafés, restaurants and bars

Bistro de Pompe

Kleine Sint Amandsstraat 2 ☎ 050/61 66 18. Tues–Sun 11.30am–9.30pm. Occupying an attractive old house close to the Markt, this modern but cosy restaurant offers a well-selected menu of fusion dishes including tasty salads, pastas and fresh grilled fish plus speciality wok dishes – the chicken is particularly good. Mains from €16.

Café Craenenburg

Markt 16. Daily 10am till late. Unlike the other touristy café-restaurants lining the Markt, this old-fashioned place still attracts a loyal, local clientele. With its leather and wood panelling, wooden benches and stained glass, the *Craenenburg* has the flavour of old Flanders, and although the daytime-only food is routine, it has a good range of beers, including the locally produced, tangy brown ale Brugse Tripel.

Den Amand

Sint Amandsstraat 4 ☎ 050/34 01 22. Tues & Thurs–Sun noon–3pm & 6–10pm, Wed noon–3pm. Decorated in pleasant modern style, this cosy and informal family-run restaurant offers inventive cuisine combining both French and Flemish traditions. Mains from the limited but well-chosen menu – for instance, swordfish in a seafood jus and seafood *waterzooi* (soup) – average a very reasonable €20. It's a small place, so best to book a few hours in advance.

De Garre

De Garre 1. Daily noon to midnight or 1am. Down a narrow alley off Breidelstraat between the Markt and the Burg, this cramped but charming tavern (*estaminet*) has an outstanding range of Belgian beers and tasty snacks, while classical music adds to the relaxed air. Smokers downstairs, non–smokers up above.

▲ DE GARRE

The Burg

From the east side of the Markt, Breidelstraat leads through to the city's other main square, the Burg, named after the fortress built here by the first count of Flanders, Baldwin Iron Arm, in the ninth century. The fortress disappeared centuries ago, but the Burg long remained the centre of political and ecclesiastical power, with the Stadhuis (Town Hall) – which has survived – on one side, and St Donatian's Cathedral – which hasn't – on the other. Fringing the southern half of the Burg is the city's finest architectural ensemble, including the Stadhuis and the Basilica of the Holy Blood, an especially handsome mix of late-Gothic and Renaissance styles.

Heilig Bloed Basiliek

April–Sept Mon, Tues & Thurs–Sun 9.30am–noon & 2–6pm, Wed 10am–noon; Oct–March Mon, Tues & Thurs–Sun 10am–noon & 2–4pm, Wed 10am–noon; free. The city's most important shrine, the Heilig Bloed Basiliek (The Basilica of the Holy Blood) is named after the holy relic that found its way here in the Middle Ages. The Basilica divides into two parts. Tucked away in the corner is the lower chapel, a shadowy, crypt-like affair, originally built at the start of the twelfth century to shelter another relic,

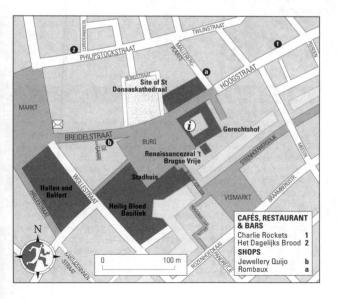

CAFÉS, RESTAURANT & BARS
Charlie Rockets 1
Het Dagelijks Brood 2
SHOPS
Jewellery Quijo b
Rombaux a

▲ BASILICA OF THE HOLY BLOOD

a piece of St Basil, one of the great figures of the early Greek Church. The chapel's heavy and simple Romanesque lines are decorated with just one relief, carved above an interior doorway and showing the baptism of Basil, in which a strange giant bird, representing the Holy Spirit, plunges into a pool of water.

The upper chapel, next door up a curving, low-vaulted staircase, was built just a few years later but has been renovated so frequently that it's impossible to make out the original structure; it also suffers from excessively rich nineteenth-century decoration. The building may be disappointing, but the large silver tabernacle that holds the rock-crystal phial of the Holy Blood is simply magnificent. The tabernacle was the gift of Albert and Isabella of Spain in 1611. The Habsburg King Philip

The Holy Blood

Local legend asserts that the Heilig Bloed (Holy Blood) was the gift of Diederik d'Alsace, a Flemish knight who distinguished himself by his bravery during the Second Crusade and was given the phial by a grateful patriarch of Jerusalem in 1150. It is, however, rather more likely that the relic was acquired during the sacking of Constantinople in 1204, when the crusaders ignored their collective job description and, instead of ridding Palestine of its Moslem rulers, simply slaughtered the Byzantines instead – hence the historical invention involving Diederik. Whatever the truth, after several weeks in Bruges the relic was found to be dry, but thereafter the dried blood proceeded to liquefy every Friday at 6pm until 1325, a miracle attested to by all sorts of church dignitaries, including Pope Clement V. The failure, in 1325, of the Holy Blood to liquefy prompted all sorts of conjecture – did it mean that Bruges had lost favour in the eyes of God? – but the phial, or more exactly its dried contents, remain an object of veneration even today, not least on Ascension Day, when it is carried through the town in a colourful but solemn procession, the Heilig-Bloedprocessie.

II of Spain had granted control of the Spanish Netherlands (now Belgium) to his daughter Isabella and her husband Albert in 1598. Failing to learn from her father's experience, Isabella continued the long-winded war against the Protestant Dutch to the north without success and at great expense. The ducal couple also persecuted those Protestants who remained in their fiefdom and exalted the Catholic faith, the tabernacle being but one example.

The phial itself (see box oppsite) is one of the holiest relics in medieval Europe, purporting to contain a few drops of blood and water washed from the body of Christ by Joseph of Arimathea. The superb reliquary that holds the phial when it's paraded through town during the Heilig-Bloedprocessie is displayed in the tiny treasury (same times; €1.50) next to the upper chapel. Dating from 1617, the reliquary's gold and silver superstructure is encrusted with jewels and decorated with tiny religious scenes and coats of arms. The treasury also holds an incidental collection of

vestments and lesser reliquaries plus – above the main door – a faded seventeenth-century tapestry depicting St Augustine's funeral. Here, the sea of helmeted heads, torches and pikes that surrounds the monks and abbots is very much a Catholic view of a muscular State supporting a holy Church.

The Stadhuis

Tues–Sun 9.30am–5pm; €2.50 including the Renaissancezaal 't Brugse Vrije (see p.62). Immediately to the left of the basilica, the Stadhuis (Town Hall) has a beautiful sandstone facade of 1376, though its statues of Flemish counts and countesses are much more recent. Inside, the grand, high-ceilinged entrance hall makes a suitably grand home for several ambitious nineteenth-century paintings, either romantic reworkings of the city's history designed to reassure the council of its distinguished pedigree, or didactic canvases to keep it up to the mark. The biggest is the whopping *Seven Works of Mercy* by Henri Dobbelaere (1829–1885), but the most original, at the foot of the stairs, is Camille van Camp's

PLACES The Burg

▲ THE STADHUIS

(1834–1891) dramatic *Death of Mary of Burgundy* – referring to a hunting accident which polished the young duchess off in 1482.

Upstairs, the magnificent Gothic Hall of 1400 has been restored in style, its ceiling, a vibrant mixture of maroon, dark brown, black and gold, dripping pendant arches like decorated stalactites. The ribs of the arches converge in twelve circular vault-keys, showing scenes from the New Testament, though they're hard to see without binoculars. Down below – and much easier to view – are the sixteen fancy gilded corbels which support them. These represent the months and the four elements, beginning in the left-hand corner beside the chimney with January (inscribed "*Winter*") and continuing clockwise

right round the hall; the gilded chariots of Air and Earth follow June ("*Lentemaand*"), Fire and Water come after September ("*Herfst*"). The wall frescoes were commissioned in 1895 to illustrate the history of the town – or rather history as the council wanted to recall it. The largest scene, commemorating the victory over the French at the Battle of the Golden Spurs in 1302, has lots of noble knights hurrahing, though it's hard to take this seriously when you look at the dogs, one of which clearly has a mismatch between its body and head.

Next door to the Gothic Hall is the historical room, where a routine display of miscellaneous artefacts, including navigational aids and the old, seven-lock municipal treasure chest, is partly redeemed by two finely executed, sixteenth-century city maps.

Renaissancezaal 't Brugse Vrije

Tues–Sun 9.30am–12.30pm & 1.30–5pm; €2.50 including the Stadhuis.
Just along from the Stadhuis is the Paleis van het Brugse Vrije (Mansion of the Liberty of Bruges), whose demure exterior belies its distinguished history. Established in the Middle Ages, the Liberty of Bruges was a territorial subdivision of Flanders which enjoyed extensive delegated powers, controlling its own finances and judiciary. Power was exercised by a council of aldermen and it was they who demolished most of the original Gothic building in the early eighteenth century – before the occupying French army abolished them in 1795. Today the building is home to the municipal archives office, but the original *Schepenkamer* (Aldermen's Room) has survived

▲ GOTHIC HALL, STADHUIS

▲ PALEIS VAN HET BRUGSE VRIJE

and this – now known as the Renaissancezaal 't Brugse Vrije (Renaissance Hall of the Liberty of Bruges) – boasts an enormous marble and oak chimneypiece. A fine example of Renaissance carving, it was completed in 1531 under the direction of Lancelot Blondeel, to celebrate the defeat of the French at the battle of Pavia in 1525 and the advantageous Treaty of Cambrai that followed. A paean of praise to the Habsburgs, the work is dominated by figures of Emperor Charles V and his Austrian and Spanish relatives, each person identified by both the free leaflet and the audio-guide, although it's the trio of bulbous codpieces that really catch the eye. The alabaster frieze running below the carvings was a caution for the Liberty's magistrates, who held their

Charles the Good and Galbert of Bruges

In 1127, St Donaaskathedraal witnessed an event that shocked the whole of Bruges, when the Count of Flanders, Charles the Good, was murdered while he was at prayer in the choir. A gifted and far-sighted ruler, Charles eschewed foreign entanglements in favour of domestic matters – unlike most of his predecessors – and improved the lot of the poor, trying to ensure a regular supply of food and controlling prices in times of shortage, and it was this, along with his piety, that earned Charles his sobriquet. The count's attempts to curb his leading vassals brought him into conflict with the powerful Erembald clan, however. The Erembalds had no intention of submitting to Charles, so they assassinated him and took control of the city. Their success was, however, short-lived. Supporters of Charles rallied and the murderers took refuge in the tower of St Donatian's, from where they were winkled out and promptly dispatched.

Shocked by the murder, one of Charles's clerks, a certain Galbert of Bruges, decided to write a detailed journal of the events that led up to the assassination and the bloody chaos that ensued. Unlike other contemporary source materials, the journal had no sponsor, which makes it a uniquely honest account of events, admittedly from the perspective of the count's entourage, with Galbert criticizing many of the city's leading figures, clergy and nobles alike. Galbert's journal provides a fascinating insight into twelfth-century Bruges and it's well written too (in a wordy sort of way) – as in the account of Charles' death: "when the count was praying … then at last, after so many plans and oaths and pacts among themselves, those wretched traitors … slew the count, who was struck down with swords and run through again and again". The full text is reprinted in *The Murder of Charles the Good* (University of Toronto Press).

courts here. In four panels, it relates the then familiar biblical story of Susanna, in which – in the first panel – two old men surprise her bathing in her garden and threaten to accuse her of adultery if she resists their advances. Susanna does just that and the second panel shows her in court. In the third panel, Susanna is about to be put to death, but the magistrate, Daniel, interrogates the two men and uncovers their perjury. Susanna is acquitted and, in the final scene, the two men are stoned to death.

The site of St Donaaskathedraal

Dating from 1722, the plodding courtyard complex of the Gerechtshof (Law Courts), adjoining the Paleis van het Bruges Vrije, is now home to the main tourist office (see p.155). Beyond, in the northeast corner of the Burg, the modern *Crowne Plaza Hotel* marks the site of St Donaaskathedraal (St Donatian's Cathedral), which was razed by the French army of occupation in 1799. This splendid structure boasted an octagonal main building flanked by a sixteen-sided ambulatory and an imposing tower. The foundations were uncovered in 1955 but were then promptly reinterred, though there are vague plans to carry out another archeological dig and erect some sort of sign or marker.

Shops

Jewellery Quijo

Breidelstraat 18 ☎050/34 10 10, ✉info@quijo.be. Mon–Sat 9am–noon & 2–6.30pm. Made in Bruges, Quijo's designer jewellery is inventive, creative and pricey.

The characteristic "Qui-shape" was, it's claimed, inspired by the shape of the city's cobblestones and is used in their ring designs and pendants.

Rombaux

Mallebergplaats 13 ☎050/33 25 75. Mon–Fri 9am–12.30pm & 2–6.30pm, Sat 9am–6pm. The idiosyncratic facade of faded old album covers conceals all manner of musical goodies, including classical to modern CDs (with a particularly good selection of jazz and blues), plus vinyl and sheet music.

Cafés and Restaurants

Charlie Rockets

Hoogstraat 19 ☎050/33 06 60, ⓦwww.charlierockets.com. Daily 8am–4am. This American-style café-bar – or at least an approximation of it – in the same building as the eponymous hostel (see p.149) attracts a youthful clientele and serves reasonably priced Tex-Mex food (6–9.30pm). There's also a large adjoining pool room with five tables and live music every fortnight from October–November.

Het Dagelijks Brood

Philipstockstraat 21. Mon & Wed–Sat 7am–6pm, Sun 8am–6pm. This excellent bread shop doubles as a wholefood café with one long wooden table – enforced communalism, which can be good fun – and a few smaller side-tables too. The mouthwatering home-made soup and bread makes a meal in itself for just €8, or you can chomp away on a range of snacks and cakes.

South of the Markt

The bustling area to the south the Markt holds the city's busiest shopping streets as well as many of its key buildings and most important museums. The area is at its prettiest among the old lanes near the cathedral, Salvatorskathedraal, which lays claim to be the city's most satisfying church, though the Onze Lieve Vrouwekerk, just to the south, comes a close second. There is more cutesiness in the huddle of whitewashed cottages of the Begijnhof and at the adjacent Minnewater, the so–called "Lake of Love". As for the museums, St Janshospitaal offers the exquisite medieval paintings of Hans Memling, the Gruuthuse is strong on applied art, especially tapestries and antique furniture, and the Groeninge (see p.85) holds a wonderful sample of early Flemish art.

▲ STATUE OF ST JOHN NEPOMUK

Huidenvettersplein and the Dijver

South of the Burg are the plain and sombre Doric colonnades of the Vismarkt (fish market), though they don't see much marine action nowadays. Neither are there any tanners in the huddle of picturesque houses that crimp the Huidenvettersplein, the square at the centre of the old tanners' quarter immediately to the west – a good job as the locals of yesteryear often complained of the stench.

You can buy a **combined ticket** (€15) for any five of Bruges' fourteen municipal museums – including the Stadhuis, Belfort, Groeninge, Gruuthuse and Memling. The ticket is available at any of the museums, and from the tourist office. Note that all these museums are closed on Mondays.

PLACES

South of the Markt

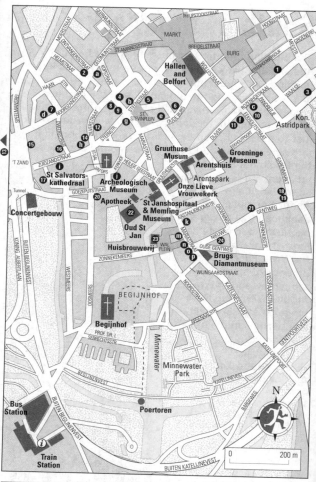

SHOPS		CAFÉS & RESTAURANTS		BARS AND CLUBS	
Bilbo	d	Cafedraal	14	B-in	22
The Chocolate Line	g	Christophe	19	De Bolero	18
Claeys	o	Den Dyver	11	Het Brugs Beertje	8
Classics	e	't Eekhoetje	10	Cactus Club	13
Decorte	a	Gran Kaffee de		Het Dreupelhuisje	9
Kasimir's Antique		Passage	16	L'Estaminet	3
Studio	c	L'Intermède	7	De Hobbit	4
Knapp Targa	h	Laurent	5	Ma Rica Rokk	15
Lady Chocolates	p	De Lotteburg	20	Huisbrouwerij De	
Leonidas	m	Lokkedize	17	Halve Mann	23
De Meester	f	Patrick Devos		Wijnbar Est	2
Neuhaus	b	"De Zilveren Pauw"	12		
Pollentier	j	De Snippe	21		
Quicke	i	Tanuki	24		
De Striep	n	De Verbeelding	6		
Sukerbuyc	k	De Visscherie	1		

▲ THE DIJVER CANAL

Nowadays, tourists converge on this pint-sized square in their droves, holing up in its bars and restaurants and snapping away at the postcard-perfect views of the Belfort (belfry) from the narrow canalside street of Rozenhoedkaai.

From here, it's a short hop west to the Wollestraat bridge, which is overlooked by a statue of the patron saint of bridges, St John Nepomuk. A fourteenth-century Bohemian priest who was purportedly thrown bound and gagged into the River Vltava for refusing to reveal the confessional secrets of the queen to her husband, King Wenceslas IV. The bridge marks the start of Dijver, the street which tracks along the canal as far as Nieuwstraat, passing the path to the first of the city's main museums, the Groeninge (see p.85), and then the Arentshuis.

The Arentshuis

Dijver 16. Tues–Sun 9.30am–5pm; €2.50, or free admission with Groeninge ticket. The Arentshuis occupies a good-looking eighteenth–century mansion with a stately porticoed entrance. Now a museum, the interior is divided into two separate sections: the ground floor is given over to temporary exhibitions, usually of fine art, while the Brangwyn Museum upstairs displays the moody sketches, etchings, lithographs, studies and paintings of the much-travelled artist Sir Frank Brangwyn (1867–1956). Born in Bruges of Welsh parents, Brangwyn flitted between Britain and Belgium, donating this sample of his work to his native town in 1936. Apprenticed to William Morris in the early 1880s and an official UK war artist in World War I, Brangwyn was nothing if not versatile, turning

▲ SKETCH BY BRANGWYN OF BEGIJNHOF, IN THE ARENTSHUIS

his hand to several different media, though his forceful drawings and sketches are much more appealing than his paintings, which often slide into sentimentality. In particular, look out for the sequence of line drawings exploring industrial themes – powerful, almost melodramatic scenes of shipbuilding, docks, construction and the like. This penchant for dark and gloomy industrial scenes bore little relationship to the British artistic trends of his day and they attracted muted reviews. Better received were his murals, whose bold designs and strong colours attracted almost universal acclaim – and a 1920s commission to turn out a series for Britain's House of Lords. In the event, these murals, whose theme was the splendour of the British Empire, ended up in Swansea Guildhall, though several of the preparatory sketches are displayed here in the Arentshuis.

Arentspark

The Arentshuis stands in the north corner of the pocket-sized Arentspark, whose brace of forlorn stone columns are all that remain of the Waterhalle, which once stood on the east side of the Markt. Demolished in 1787, the Waterhalle straddled the most central of the city's canals, with boats sailing inside the building to unload their cargoes. When part of the canal – between Jan van Eyckplein and the Dijver – was covered over in the middle of the eighteenth century, the Waterhalle became redundant; its place has mostly been taken by the main Post Office. Also in the Arentspark is the tiniest of humpbacked bridges – St Bonifaciusbrug – whose stonework is framed against a tumble of antique brick houses. One of Bruges' most picturesque (and photographed) spots, the bridge looks like the epitome of everything medieval, but in fact it was built only in 1910. Next to the far side of the bridge, a modern statue does few favours for Juan Luis Vives, a Spanish Jew and friend of Erasmus, who settled here in the early sixteenth century to avoid persecution. It was a wise decision: back in Spain his family had converted to Christianity, but even that failed to save them. His father was burnt at the stake in 1525 and his dead mother was dug up and her bones burned.

St Boni-faciusbrug spans the canal behind and between two of the city's main museums – the Arentshuis and the Gruuthuse.

▲ ST BONIFACIUSBRUG

The Gruuthuse Museum

Dijver 17. Tues–Sun 9.30am–5pm; €6 including audio-guide. Occupying a rambling mansion dating from the fifteenth century – a fine example of civil Gothic architecture – the Gruuthuse Museum takes its name from the houseowners' historical right to tax the *gruit*, the dried herb and flower mixture once added to barley during the beer-brewing process to improve the flavour. The last lord of the *gruit* died in 1492 and, after many twists, the mansion was turned into a museum to hold a hotchpotch of Flemish fine, applied and decorative arts, mostly dating from the medieval and early modern period. The museum's strongest suit is its superb collection of tapestries (see box below), mostly woven in Brussels or Bruges during the sixteenth and seventeenth centuries. Most rooms carry multilingual cards explaining the more important exhibits, but the museum can feel like a dumping ground for artefacts that no one knows much about.

The first room houses a charming set of four early seventeenth-century Bruges tapestries depicting scenes of rural merrymaking. The central characters are a shepherd and shepherdess, Gombaut and Macée, well-known folkloric figures whose various adventures were used as fables to laugh at human frailty in general – and sexual peccadilloes in particular.

Room 2 boasts a much-reproduced polychromatic

The Bruges tapestry industry

Tapestry manufacture in Bruges began in the middle of the fourteenth century. The embryonic industry soon came to be based on a dual system of workshop and outworker, the one using paid employees, the other with workers paid on a piecework basis. From the beginning, the town authorities took a keen interest in the business, ensuring consistency by a rigorous system of quality control. The other side of this interventionist policy was less palatable: wages were kept down and the workers were hardly ever able to accumulate enough capital to buy either their own looms or even the raw materials.

There were two great periods of Bruges tapestry-making, the first from the early fifteenth until the middle of the sixteenth century, the second from the 1580s to the 1790s. Tapestry production was a cross between embroidery and ordinary weaving. It consisted of interlacing a wool weft above and below the strings of a vertical linen "chain", a process similar to weaving. However, the weaver had to stop to change colour, requiring as many shuttles for the weft as he or she had colours, as in embroidery. The appearance of a tapestry was entirely determined by the weft, the design being taken from a painting – or cartoon of a painting – to which the weaver made constant reference. Standard-size tapestries took six months to make and were produced exclusively for the very wealthy. The most famous artists of the day were often involved in the preparatory paintings – Pieter Paul Rubens, Bernard van Orley and David Teniers all had tapestry commissions.

There were only two significant types of tapestry: decorative, principally verdures, showing scenes of foliage in an almost abstract way; and pictorial (the Bruges speciality) – usually variations on the same basic themes, particularly rural life, knights, hunting parties, classical gods and goddesses and religious scenes. Over the centuries, changes in style were strictly limited, though the early part of the seventeenth century saw an increased use of elaborate woven borders, an appreciation of perspective and the use of a far brighter, more varied range of colours.

terracotta bust of the Emperor Charles V, while Rooms 3 to 5 hold an enjoyable medley of Gothic furniture and woodcarvings. Upstairs, in Room 10, look out for a pair of bold and richly coloured classical tapestries, produced in Bruges in 1675 and entitled *De Zeven Vrije Kunsten* ("The Seven Free Arts"). The arts concerned – rhetoric, astrology, and so on – were considered necessary for the rounded education of a gentleman. Most intriguing, however, is the 1472 oak-panelled oratory (Room 17), which juts out from the first floor of the museum to overlook the altar of the cathedral next door. A curiously intimate room, the oratory allowed the lords of the *gruit* to worship without leaving home – a real social coup.

▲ THE GRUUTHUSE MUSEUM

Onze Lieve Vrouwekerk

Mon–Sat 9.30am–12.15pm & 1.30–5pm, Sun 1.30–5pm; free.
The Onze Lieve Vrouwekerk (The Church of Our Lady) is a rambling shambles of a building, a clamour of different dates and styles, whose brick spire is – at 122m – one of the tallest in Belgium. Entered from the south, the nave was three hundred years in the making, an architecturally discordant affair, whose thirteenth-century, grey-stone central aisle is the oldest part of the church. The central aisle blends in with the south aisle, but the later, fourteenth-century north aisle doesn't mesh at all – even the columns aren't aligned. This was the result of changing fashions, not slapdash work: the High Gothic north aisle was intended to be the start of a complete remodelling of the church, but the money ran out before the work was finished.

In the south aisle is the church's most acclaimed *objet d'art*, a delicate marble Madonna and Child by Michelangelo. Purchased by a Bruges merchant, this was the only one of Michelangelo's works to leave Italy during the artist's lifetime and it had a significant influence on the painters then working in Bruges, though its present setting – beneath gloomy stone walls – is hardly prepossessing.

Michelangelo apart, the most interesting part of the church is the chancel (€2.50), beyond the black-and-white marble rood screen. Here you'll find the mausoleums of Charles the Bold and his daughter Mary of Burgundy (see box opposite), two exquisite examples of Renaissance carving whose side-panels are decorated with coats of arms connected by the most intricate of floral designs. The royal figures are enhanced in the detail, from the helmet and gauntlets placed gracefully by Charles' side to the pair of watchful dogs nestled at Mary's feet. The hole dug by archeologists beneath the mausoleums during the 1970s (see box below) was never filled in and mirrors now give sight of Mary's coffin along with the burial vaults of several unknown medieval dignitaries, several of which have been moved to the Lanchals Chapel (see p.72). The coats of arms above the choir stalls are those of the knights of the Order of the Golden Fleece (see box on p.75), who met here in 1468.

Just across the ambulatory from the mausoleums, the Lanchals Chapel holds the

▲ MICHELANGELO'S MADONNA AND CHILD, ONZE LIEVE VROUWEKERK

The earthly remains of Mary of Burgundy and Charles the Bold

The last independent rulers of Flanders were **Charles the Bold**, the Duke of Burgundy, and his daughter **Mary of Burgundy**, both of whom died in unfortunate circumstances, Charles during the siege of the French city of Nancy in 1477, Mary after a riding accident in 1482, when she was only 25. Mary was married to Maximilian, a Habsburg prince and future Holy Roman Emperor, who inherited her territories on her death. Thus, at a dynastic stroke, Flanders was incorporated into the Habsburg empire.

In the sixteenth century, the Habsburgs relocated to Spain, but they were keen to emphasize their connections with – and historical authority over – Flanders, the richest part of their expanding empire. Nothing did this quite as well as the ceremonial burial – or re-burial – of bits of royal body. Mary was safely ensconced in Bruges' Onze Lieve Vrouwekerk, but the body of Charles was in a makeshift grave in Nancy. The emperor Charles V, the great grandson of Charles the Bold, had – or thought he had – this body exhumed and carried to Bruges, where it was reinterred next to Mary.

There were, however, persistent rumours that the French, traditional enemies of the Habsburgs, had deliberately handed over a dud skeleton, specifically one of the knights who died in the same engagement. In the 1970s, archeologists had a bash at solving the mystery. They dug beneath Charles and Mary's mausoleums in the Onze Lieve Vrouwekerk but, amongst the assorted tombs, failed to authoritatively identify either the body or even the tomb of Charles; Mary proved more tractable, with her skeleton confirming the known details of her hunting accident. Buried alongside her also was the urn which contained the heart of her son, Philip the Fair, placed here in 1506.

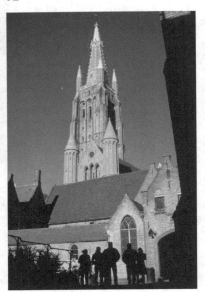

▲ ONZE LIEVE VROUWEKERK

medieval burial vaults, each plastered with lime mortar. The inside walls of the vaults sport brightly coloured grave frescoes, a type of art which flourished hereabouts from the late thirteenth to the middle of the fifteenth century. The iconography is fairly consistent, with the long sides mostly bearing one, sometimes two, angels apiece, with most of them shown swinging thuribles (the vessels in which incense is burnt during religious ceremonies). Typically, the short sides show the Crucifixion and a Virgin and Child and there's sometimes an image of the dead person or his/her patron saint too. The background decoration is more varied, with crosses, stars and dots all making appearances as well as two main sorts of flower – roses and bluebells. The frescoes were painted freehand and executed at great speed – Flemings were then buried on the day they died – hence the immediacy of the work.

imposing Baroque gravestone of Pieter Lanchals, a one-time Habsburg official who was executed by the citizens of Bruges in 1488. Legend asserts that he was beheaded for his opposition to Maximilian's temporary imprisonment in the Craenenburg (see p.53) and that, to atone for its crime, Bruges was later obliged to introduce swans to its canals. Both tales are, however, fabrications, seemingly invented in the nineteenth century: Lanchals actually had his head lopped off for being corrupt and was soon forgotten by his erstwhile sponsor, while the swan story seems to have originated with the swan that adorns his gravestone – the bird was the man's emblem, appropriately enough, as his name means "long neck".

In front of the Lanchals gravestone are three relocated

St Janshospitaal

The sprawling complex of St Janshospitaal sheltered the sick until the nineteenth century, and the oldest part – at the front on Mariastraat, behind two church-like gable ends – has recently been turned into a slick museum (see opposite). A narrow passageway on the north side of the museum leads from Mariastraat to the other parts of the complex, beginning with the hospital's old Apotheek (apothecary; Tues–Sun 9.30am–5pm; free), which comes complete with rows of antique porcelain, earthenware and glass jars. The passageway then continues onto a relatively modern, elongated annexe that has been turned into an exhibition-cum-shopping centre and is called – rather confusingly – Oud St-Jan.

The St Janshospitaal museum

Tues–Sun 9.30am–5pm; €8 including audio-guide. St Janshospitaal museum divides into two, with one large section – in the former hospital ward – exploring the historical background to the hospital through documents, paintings and religious *objets d'art*; and a second, smaller section (see below), sited in the old hospital chapel, devoted to six works by Hans Memling. In both, the labelling is minimal, though the audio-guide provides copious background information. Highlights of the larger section include Jan Beerblock's *The Wards of St Janshospitaal* (audio-guide no.27; exhibit no.66), a minutely detailed painting of the hospital ward in the late eighteenth century. Here you can see what the ward actually looked like, the patients tucked away in row upon row of tiny, cupboard-like beds. There were 150 beds in total divided into three sections – one for women, one for men and the third for the dying. Other noteworthy paintings include an exquisite *Deposition* (audio–guide no.36; exhibit no.138), a late fifteenth-century version of an original by Rogier van der Weyden, and a stylish, intimately observed diptych (audioguide no.38; exhibit no.153) by Jan Provoost (see p.89), with portraits of Christ and the donor on the front and a skull on the back.

The Memling collection

Adjoining the former hospital ward, the hospital chapel now houses six works by Hans Memling (1430–1494). Born near Frankfurt, Memling spent most of his working life in Bruges, where he was taught by Rogier van der Weyden (see p.86). He adopted much of his tutor's style and stuck to the detailed symbolism of his contemporaries, but his painterly manner was distinctly restrained, often pious and grave. His figures also had a velvet-like quality that greatly appealed to the city's burghers, whose enthusiasm made Memling a rich man. Of the six works on display, the most unusual is the *Reliquary of St Ursula*, comprising a miniature wooden Gothic church painted with the story of St Ursula. Six panels show Ursula and her ten companions on their way to Rome, only to be

▲ ST JANSHOSPITAAL MUSEUM

massacred by Huns as they passed through Germany. It is, however, the mass of incidental detail that makes the reliquary so enchanting – a wonderful evocation of the late medieval world. Equally delightful is the *Mystical Marriage of St Catherine*, the middle panel of a large triptych depicting St Catherine, who represents contemplation, receiving a ring from the baby Jesus to seal their spiritual union. In the background, behind St John, is the giant wooden crane that once dominated the Kraanplein (see p.95). Across the chapel are two more Memling triptychs, a *Lamentation* and an *Adoration of the Magi*, in which there's a gentle nervousness in the approach of the Magi, here shown as the kings of Spain, Arabia and Ethiopia.

In the adjoining side-chapel, Memling's skill as a portraitist is demonstrated by his *Virgin and Martin van Nieuwenhove* diptych, in which the eponymous merchant has the flush of youth and a hint of arrogance. His lips pout, his hair cascades down to his shoulders and he is dressed in the most fashionable of

doublets – no Bruges merchant wanted to appear too pious. Opposite, the Virgin gets the full stereotypical treatment from the oval face and the almond-shaped eyes through to full cheeks, thin nose and bunched lower lip. There's more fine face-work opposite in Memling's *Portrait of a Woman*, where the richly dressed subject stares dreamily into the middle distance, her hands – in a superb optical illusion – seeming to clasp the picture frame.

Archeological Museum

Mariastraat 36a. Tues–Sun 9.30am–12.30pm & 1.30–5pm; €2. Often ignored, the city's Archeological Museum (Archeologisch Museum) is admittedly quite modest – and most of the labelling is in Dutch – but it does have several mildly diverting displays, beginning with a small section on the nature of archeology itself. Upstairs, the first floor has a substantial section devoted to the city's medieval tanners, featuring an assortment of decrepit leather shoes recovered from a number of digs. On the same floor are several piles of accumulated artefacts retrieved from waste pits and cesspits – these are displayed in the form they were unearthed, but without the attached detritus. There are also a couple of cabinets displaying a miscellany of ancient artefacts, pottery shards, stone axes and, pick of the bunch, the battered remains of several Merovingian swords and buckles.

St Salvatorskathedraal

Mon 2–5.45pm, Tues–Fri 9–11.45am & 2–5.45pm, Sat 9–11.45am & 2–3.30pm, Sun 9–10.15am & 2–5pm; free. St Salvatorskathedraal (Holy

▲ DETAIL FROM *VIRGIN AND MARTIN VAN NIEUWENHOVE* DIPTYCH BY MEMLING

Saviour's Cathedral) is a bulky Gothic edifice that mostly dates from the late thirteenth century, though the Flamboyant Gothic ambulatory was added some two centuries later. A parish church for most of its history, it was only made a cathedral in 1834 following the destruction of St Donatian's (see p.64) by the French. This change of status prompted lots of ecclesiastical rumblings – nearby Onze Lieve Vrouwekerk (see p.70) was bigger and its spire higher – and when part of St Salvators went up in smoke in 1839, the opportunity was taken to make its tower higher and grander in a romantic rendition of the Romanesque style.

Now nearing the end of a long-term refurbishment, the cathedral's nave has recently emerged from centuries of

▲ ST SALVATORSKATHEDRAAL

accumulated grime, but it remains a cheerless, cavernous affair. The star turn is the set of eight paintings by Jan van

The Order of the Golden Fleece

Philip the Good, the Duke of Burgundy, invented the Order of the Golden Fleece in 1430 on the occasion of his marriage to Isabella of Portugal. Duke since 1419, Philip had spent much of his time curbing the power of the Flemish cities – including Bruges – but he was too economically dependent on them to feel entirely secure. To bolster his position, the duke was always looking for ways to emphasize his aristocratic credentials and add lustre to his dynasty, hence his creation of the Order of the Golden Fleece, an exclusive, knightly club – with himself as Grand Master – that harked back to the (supposed) age of chivalry. The choice of the name was a complimentary nod both to the wool weavers of Flanders, who provided him with most of his money, and to the legends of classical Greece. In the Greek story, a winged ram named Chrysomallus – gifted with the power of speech and a golden fleece – saved the life of Phrixus, presented him with his fleece and then flew off to become the constellation of Aries (it was this same fleece that Jason and the Argonauts later sought to recover). The Order's emblem – a golden ram – can be seen on portraits and hatchments around the city.

Philip stipulated that membership of the Order be restricted to "noblemen in name and proven in valour ... born and raised in legitimate wedlock". He promptly picked the membership and appointed himself Grand Master. It was all something of a con trick, but it went down a treat and the 24 knights who were offered membership duly turned up at the first meeting in Lille in 1431. Thereafter, the Order met fairly regularly, with Bruges and Ghent being two favourite venues, gathering together for some mutual back-slapping, feasting and the exchange of presents. However, when the Habsburgs swallowed up Burgundy in the late fifteenth century, the Order was rendered obsolete and the title "Grand Master" became just one of the family's many dynastic trinkets.

Orley displayed in and around the transepts. Commissioned in the 1730s, the paintings were used for the manufacture of a matching set of tapestries from a Brussels workshop and, remarkably enough, these have survived too and hang in sequence in the choir and transepts. Each of the eight scenes is a fluent, dramatic composition featuring a familiar episode from the life of Christ – from the Nativity to the Resurrection – complete with a handful of animals, including a remarkably determined Palm Sunday donkey.

Entered from the nave, the cathedral treasury (daily except Sat 2–5pm; €2.50) occupies the adjoining neo-Gothic chapter house, whose nine rooms are packed with ecclesiastical tackle, from religious paintings and statues through to an assortment of reliquaries, vestments and croziers. The labelling is poor, however, so it's a good idea to pick up the English-language mini-guide at the entrance. Room B holds the treasury's finest painting, a gruesome, oak-panel triptych, *The Martyrdom of St Hippolytus*, by Dieric Bouts (1410–1475) and Hugo van der Goes (died 1482). The right panel depicts the Roman Emperor Decius, a notorious persecutor of Christians, trying to persuade the priest Hippolytus to abjure his faith. He fails, and in the central panel Hippolytus is pulled to pieces by four horses.

Brugs Diamantmuseum

Katelijnestraat 43 ☎050/34 20 56, ⓦ www.diamondmuseum.be. Daily 10.30am–5.30pm; €6. The mildly entertaining Brugs Diamantmuseum (Bruges Diamond Museum) tracks through the history of the city's diamond industry in a series of smartly presented displays. There are several examples of diamonds and their settings as well as daily demonstrations of diamond polishing at 12.15pm.

Huisbrouwerij De Halve Maan

Walplein 26 ☎050/33 26 97, ⓦ www.halvemaan.be. Frequent guided tours daily April–Sept 11am–4pm; Oct–March 11am & 3pm; €3.70, including a glass of beer. The Brugs Diamantmuseum stands opposite the east end of Wijngaardstraat, whose antique terrace houses are crammed with souvenir shops, bars and restaurants. This street and its immediate surroundings heave with tourists, unpleasantly so in summer, with many trooping off to the Walplein, where the brewery Huisbrouwerij De Halve Maan (Half Moon Brewery) offers 45-minute guided tours; the free beer on offer is Straffe Hendrik, the leading local brew.

▲ HUISBROUWERIJ BREWERY DE HALVE MAAN

The Begijnhof

Daily 9am–6pm or sunset; free. Much more appealing, if just as over-visited, is the Begijnhof, just off – and over the bridge from – the west end of Wijngaardstraat, where a rough circle of old and infinitely pretty whitewashed houses surrounds a central green. The best time to visit is in spring, when a carpet of daffodils pushes up between the wispy elms, creating one of the most photographed scenes in Bruges. There were once *begijnhofs* all over Belgium, and this is

▲ BEGIJNHOF

one of the few to have survived in good nick. They date back to the twelfth century, when a Liège priest, a certain Lambert le Bègue, encouraged widows and unmarried women to live in communities, the better to do pious acts, especially caring for the sick. These communities were different from convents in so far as the inhabitants – the beguines (*begijns*) – did not have to take conventual vows and had the right to return to the secular world if they wished. Margaret, Countess of Flanders, founded Bruges' *begijnhof* in 1245 and, although most of the houses now standing date from the eighteenth century, the medieval layout has survived intact, preserving the impression of the *begijnhof* as a self-contained village, with access controlled through two large gates.

The houses are still in private hands, but, with the beguines long gone, they are now occupied by Benedictine nuns, who you'll see flitting around in

their habits. Only one is open to the public – the Begijnenhuisje (March–Nov Mon–Fri 10am– noon & 1.45–5.30/6pm, Sat 10am–noon, Sun 10.45am–noon & 1.45–5.30/6pm; €2), a pint-sized celebration of the simple life of the beguines. The prime exhibit here is the *schapraai*, a traditional beguine's cupboard, which was a frugal combination of dining table, cutlery cabinet and larder.

The Minnewater

Facing the more southerly of the *begijnhof*'s two gates is the Minnewater, often hyped as the city's "Lake of Love". The tag certainly gets the canoodlers going, but in fact the lake – more a large pond – started life as a city harbour. The distinctive stone lock house at the head of the Minnewater recalls its earlier function, though it's actually a very fanciful nineteenth-century reconstruction of the medieval original. The Poertoren, on the west bank at the far end of the lake, is more authentic, its brown brickwork dating from 1398 and once part of the city wall. This is where the city kept its gunpowder – hence the name, "powder tower".

Beside the Poertoren, a footbridge spans the southern end of the Minnewater to reach the leafy expanse of Minnewaterpark, which trails north back towards the *begijnhof*.

Shops

Bilbo

Noordzandstraat 82 ℡ 050/33 40 11. Mon–Sat 10am–6.30pm. The most popular CD shop in town, especially amongst under-25s, thanks to its bargain-basement prices and large selection of mainstream pop and rock – although there's not much in the way of service or presentation.

The Chocolate Line

Simon Stevinplein 19 ℡ 050/34 10 90, ⓦ www.thechocolateline .be. Tues–Sat 9.30am–6pm, Mon & Sun 10.30am–6pm. Probably the best chocolate shop in town, serving up quality chocolates, handmade on the premises using natural ingredients – not surprisingly, it's more expensive than most of its plethora of rivals. Chocolate truffles and figurines are a speciality. Boxes

of mixed chocolates are sold in various sizes: a 250g box costs €8; a small box of six chocolates is €4.

Claeys

Katelijnestraat 54 ℡ 050/33 98 19, ⓦ www.claeysantique.com. Daily 9am–6.30pm. Diane Claeys studied lace history and design in various museums in Europe before opening this shop in 1980. She now sells handmade, antique-style lace, from handkerchiefs to edging and tablecloths, and also sometimes organizes lace exhibitions here.

Classics

Oude Burg 32 ℡ 050/33 90 58. Tues–Sat 10am–noon & 2–6pm. A mixed bag of an art shop selling everything from fine art, tapestries and antiques to more modern objects, in a traditional style, collected from around the world. Also stocks Indian textiles. Affordable prices.

Decorte

Noordzandstraat 23 ℡ 050/33 46 07. Mon–Sat 9am–12.30pm & 1.30–6pm. Stationery nirvana, with magnificent fountain pens, coloured pencils, ink pots, wrapping paper, cards and writing paper, at prices to suit every budget.

Kasimir's Antique Studio

Rozenhoedkaai 3 ℡ 050/34 56 61. Mon–Sat 10.30am–12.30pm & 2–6pm.

Markets

Bruges has two food and general goods markets, a pretty average one on the Markt (Wed 8am–1pm) and a bigger and better version on 't Zand (Sat 8am–1pm). There's also a flea market along the Dijver and on the neighbouring Vismarkt (mid-March to mid-Nov Sat & Sun 10am–6pm), though there are more souvenir and craft stalls here than bric-à-brac places, and the tourist crowds also mean that bargains are few and far between – if you're after a bargain, you might consider popping over to the much larger flea markets in Ghent (see p.131).

Antiques don't come cheap in Bruges, and Kasimir's is no exception, but the old furniture on sale here is first-rate, and there's an interesting assortment of old knick-knacks – from ceramics to glassware – too.

Knapp Targa

Zuidzandstraat 9 and across the street at no. 18–26 ☎050/33 31 27, ⓦwww.knapp-targa.be. Mon–Sat 10am–6.30pm. Arguably the most enjoyable fashion shop in town, Knapp Targa's chic repertoire of top-quality clothes ranges from the adventurous – or even challenging – to the classic, with labels including Burberry, DKNY, Paul Smith and Coast. They also have a branch to the west of the city centre at Gistelsesteenweg 22–28 (daily 10am–6.30pm, closed Mon am & Sun pm ☎050/33 07 44). Gistelsesteenweg runs west from Canadaplein, which abuts the Smedenpoort city gate.

Lady Chocolates

Katelijnestraat 60 ☎050/33 78 40. Mon–Sat 10am–6pm, closed Tues & Thurs Jan to mid-Feb. This place doesn't have quite as big a selection as other shops along this street, but it does have some of the best-priced pre-packed boxes (€10.90 for 1kg). The owner also runs regular promotions and stocks a wide choice of chocolate figures. Self-service individual chocolates cost €3 for 125kg and €17 for 1kg.

Leonidas

Katelijnestraat 24 ☎050/34 69 41, ⓦwww.leonidas.com. Mon–Sat 9am–7pm, Sun 10am–6pm. Part of the popular Belgian chain and offering a large selection of pralines and candy confectionery, including Bruges rock, all at reasonable prices (€3.72 for 250g and €14.86 for 1kg), though they're more sugary than more exclusive rivals. As with all chocolate shops along Katelijnestraat, expect queues in the summer.

De Meester

Dijver 2 ☎050/33 29 52. Mon–Sat 8.30am–noon & 1.30–6.30pm. De Meester (aka De Brugse Boekhandel) is good for books about Bruges, both past and present, and sells a wide range of city maps. It's also reasonably strong on other topics, notably historical subjects, literature from home and abroad, cookery and gardening.

Neuhaus

Steenstraat 66 ☎050/33 15 30, ⓦwww.neuhaus.be. Mon–Thurs 10am–6.30pm, Fri & Sat 10am–7pm, Sun 1.30–6pm. Belgium's best chocolate chain sells superb and beautifully presented chocolates. Check out their specialities such as the handmade Caprices – pralines stuffed with crispy nougat, fresh cream and soft-centred chocolate – and the delicious Manons – stuffed white chocolates, which come with fresh cream, vanilla and coffee fillings. Prices are €9.75 for 250g, €19.50 for 500g or €39 for a 1kg box.

Pollentier

Sint Salvatorskerkhof 8 ☎050/33 18 04. Tues–Fri 2–6pm, Sat 10am–noon & 2–6pm. This antiquarian hideaway specializes in old and contemporary prints, and also offers a framing service. Seascapes, hunting scenes and Bruges cityscapes predominate, but there are many other subjects as well.

Quicke

Zuidzandstraat 21 ☎ 050/33 23 00,
🌐 www.quicke.be. Mon & Sat 10am–
6.30pm, Tues–Thurs 9.30am–6.30pm.
The top shoe shop in Bruges,
Quicke showcases the great
European seasonal collections,
featuring exclusive designers
such as Prada and Mui Miu.
Naturally it's expensive.

De Striep

Katelijnestraat 42 ☎ 050/33 71 12.
Mon 1.30–7pm, Tues–Sat 9am–
12.30pm & 1.30–7pm, Sun 2–6pm.
The only comic-strip specialist
in town, stocking everything
from run-of-the-mill cheapies
to collector items in Flemish,
French and even English.

Sukerbuyc

Katelijnestraat 5 ☎ 050/33 08
87, 🌐 www.sukerbuyc.com. Daily
8.30am–6.30pm. This family-run
chocolate shop offers over 90
types of handmade chocolates,
including their speciality
marzipan fruits. Prices are
considerably higher than some
of their rivals (€6 for 250g,
€24 for 1kg, and 100g bags for
€2.40), but there's no disputing
the quality.

Cafés and restaurants

Cafedraal

Zilverstraat 38 ☎ 050/34 08 45,
🌐 www.cafedraal.be. Mon–Sat
11am–1am, food served till 10.30pm.
Fashionable and justifiably
popular restaurant decked out
in ersatz medieval style, with
a big open fire in winter and
an outside garden terrace in
summer. The menu runs the
gamut of French and Flemish
dishes, but it's hard to beat
the North Sea bouillabaisse or
the lobster and veal cooked in
mustard. Main courses around
€20.

Christophe

Garenmarkt 34 ☎ 050/34 48 92. Mon
& Thurs–Sun 7pm–1am. Convivial,
pocket–sized restaurant with
attractive, informal decor and
a small but choice menu of
French and Flemish dishes.
Daily specials are a feature
and prices are very reasonable
– with main courses averaging
around €20.

▲ DEN DYJVER RESTAURANT

Den Dyver

Dijver 5 ☎ 050/33 60 69. Daily noon–2pm & 6.30–9pm, closed Wed & Thurs lunch. Top-flight restaurant specializing in traditional Flemish dishes cooked in beer – the quail and rabbit are magnificent, though the seafood runs them close. The decor is plush and antique, with tapestries on the wall beneath an ancient wood-beam ceiling. The service is attentive, but not unduly so, and the only real negative is the Muzak, which can be tiresome. Popular with an older clientele. Reservations advised. Mains around €25.

▲ LOKKEDIZE CAFÉ-BAR

't Eekhoetje

Eekhoutstraat 3 ☎ 050/34 89 79. Daily except Wed 7.30am–7.30pm. Bright and airy tearoom, with a small courtyard, just a short walk from the crowds of Huidenvettersplein. The efficient and friendly staff serve a good selection of tasty snacks and light meals such as omelettes, pasta and toasties; there's also a licensed bar and a sandwich deli offering cold fillings and hot pasties. Takeaway available.

Gran Kaffee de Passage

Dweersstraat 26 ☎ 050/34 02 32. Daily 6pm–midnight. This lively café is extremely popular with backpackers, many of whom have bunked down in the adjacent *Passage Hostel* (see p.149). Serves up a good and filling line in Flemish food, with many dishes cooked in beer, as well as mussels and vegetarian options. Not much in the way of frills, but then main courses only cost about €10.

Laurent

Steenstraat 79c. Daily 9am–5.30pm. Cheap and cheerful café-restaurant metres from the cathedral. No points for decor or atmosphere, but the snacks are filling and fresh and the pancakes first-rate. Very popular with locals.

L'Intermède

Wulfhagestraat 3 ☎ 050/33 16 74. Tues–Sat noon–1.30pm & 7–9.30pm. Tastefully decorated and very chic little restaurant serving exquisite French cuisine with a Flemish twist. Prices are reasonable and it's away from the tourist zone – which is very much to its advantage. Mains €18–24.

Lokkedize

Korte Vuldersstraat 33 ☎ 050/33 44 50. Wed & Thurs 7pm–midnight, Fri & Sat 6pm–1am, Sun 6pm–midnight. Attracting a youthful crowd, this sympathetic café-bar – all subdued lighting, fresh flowers and jazz music – serves up a good line in Mediterranean food, with main courses averaging around €9 and bar snacks from €4.

De Lotteburg

Goezeputstraat 43 ⌾050/33 75 35, ⓦwww.lotteburg.com. Wed–Fri & Sun noon–2pm & 7–9.30pm, Sat 7–9.30pm; last orders 30min before closing. Usually closed for holidays for two weeks in Jan and again in late July. One of the town's two outstanding fish restaurants (along with *De Visscherie*; see opposite), this very smart and formal little place has a superb menu, with imaginative, carefully prepared dishes like shrimps and truffle oil, sole and mushrooms. The set menus cost an arm and a leg, but main courses average €30–35 – expensive, but well worth it. Lunches cost in the region of €30. Don't miss the fish soup. Reservations essential.

▲ DE VISSCHERIE

Patrick Devos "De Zilveren Pauw"

Zilverstraat 41 ⌾050/33 55 66, ⓦwww.patrickdevos.be. Mon–Fri noon–1.30pm & 7–9pm, Sat 7–9pm. One of Bruges' premier restaurants, whose speciality is themed meals, such as Art Nouveau lunches and belle époque dinners. These are the creations of Patrick Devos, a great name in Belgian cooking and the designer of such treats as jelly of seafood perfumed with garlic, and duck with rhubarb. A full meal will set you back at least €50, main courses from about €30. It's a formal – some would say staid – establishment, and reservations are essential.

De Snippe

Nieuwe Gentweg 53 ⌾050/33 70 70, ⓦwww.desnippe.be. Mon 7–9.30pm Tues–Sat noon–2.30pm & 7–9.30pm . The serious-looking, eighteenth-century facade of the *Hotel De Snippe* barely hints at the cultured extravagance that lies within, all stiff flowers, heavy drapes and chandeliers. The hotel restaurant is one of the best in town, offering *haute cuisine* with an especially strong line in langoustines. Main courses €30–35.

Tanuki

Oude Gentweg 1 ⌾050/34 75 12. Wed–Sun noon–2pm & 6.30–9.30pm; closed two weeks in Jan & July. The best Japanese restaurant in town and a possibly welcome break from the creamy sauces of Belgian cuisine. The menu features all the usual Japanese favourites – noodles, sushi and sashimi – and prices are very reasonable, with most dishes around €12.50.

De Verbeelding

Oude Burg 26 ☎050/33 82 94.
Mon–Sat 11am–11pm. Low-key,
amenable café-bar serving a
reasonably satisfying range of
salads, pastas and tapas. Few
would say the food was brilliant,
but it is inexpensive and – at its
best – very tasty. Main courses
around €10, half that for tapas.
Handy for the Markt.

De Visscherie

Vismarkt 8 ☎050/33 02 12, ⓦwww
.visscherie.be. Daily except Tues noon–
2pm & 7–10pm; closed for holidays
from late Nov to mid-Dec. This is the
second of the city's excellent
seafood restaurants, but unlike
its rival – *De Lotteburg*, opposite
– it manages to be smart and
relaxed at the same time. A
well-presented and imaginative
menu features such delights as
a spectacularly tasty fish soup
(€15), seafood *waterzooi* (€25)
and cod cooked in traditional
Flemish style (€30). The
restaurant occupies a spacious
nineteenth-century mansion
a short walk south of the
Burg, but the decor has some
intriguing modern touches
– small sculptures and so on
– and the chairs are supremely
comfortable.

Bars and clubs

B-in

Mariastraat 38 ☎050/34 56 76,
ⓦwww.b-in.be. Daily except Tues
10am–3am, Fri & Sat until 5am.
The coolest place in town, this
recently opened bar-club is
kitted out in attractive modern
style with low, comfy seating
and an eye-grabbing mix of
coloured fluorescent tubes and
soft ceiling lights. Guest DJs play
funky, uplifting house, and there
are reasonably priced drinks

and cocktails and a relaxed and
friendly crowd. Gets going
about 11pm. Free entry.

De Bolero

Garenmarkt 32. Mon & Wed–Fri 10pm–
4am, Sat 4pm–4am. Currently the
only gay and lesbian bar/club
in town, hosting regular dance
evenings with a wide range of
sounds, from Abba to house.
Entrance is free and the drinks
are very reasonably priced.

Het Brugs Beertje

Kemelstraat 5. Daily except Wed
4pm–1am. This small and friendly
speciality beer bar claims a stock
of three hundred beers, which
aficionados reckon is one of the
best selections in Belgium, and
there are tasty snacks too, such
as cheeses and salad. Popular
with backpackers.

Cactus Club

Magdalenastraat 27 ☎050/33 20 14,
ⓦwww.cactusmusic.be. Recently
moved to a new location in
Magdalenastraat, the *Cactus
Club* organizes eight or so
events throughout the year
(admission usually €8–14)
– see the website for upcoming
events. They also host the
long-established three-day
Cactusfestival held (second
weekend of July; see p.159) and
the annual Klinkers Festival (see
p.159), a free two-week cultural
jamboree held in the summer
around the Burg.

Het Dreupelhuisje

Kemelstraat 9. Daily except Tues
6pm–2am. Tiny, laid-back
and eminently agreeable bar
specializing in *jenever* (gin) and
advocaat, of which it has an
outstanding range. Two doors
down from *Het Brugs Beertje* (see
above).

De Hobbit

Kemelstraat 8. Wed–Sun 4pm–1am.
Kemelstraat is short, but it's
home to two great bars, *Het
Dreupelhuisje* and *Het Brugs
Beertje* (see p.83). If they're full
– as they often are – *De Hobbit*
is a third (reserve) option, a
laid-back, student-style café-
bar that's busy till late. There's
also inexpensive food available,
and many people eat here, but
the quality and the service are
patchy.

Huisbrouwerij De Halve Mann

Walplein 26 ☎050/33 26 97, ✆www.
halvemaan.be. Daily 10am–6pm.
The big and breezy bar of
the Huisbrouwerij De Halve
Maan brewery is a popular
tourist spot, thanks to its leafy
courtyard and guided brewery
tours (see p.76). The house
speciality – a sharp pale ale
called Straffe Hendrik (Strong
Henry) – is one of Flanders'
better brews.

L'Estaminet

Park 5 ☎050/33 09 16. Daily except
Thurs 11.30am–1am or later. Groovy
neighbourhood café-bar with
a relaxed feel and (for Bruges)
a diverse and cosmopolitan
clientele. Rickety furniture both
inside and on the large outside
terrace adds to the flavour of
the place, as does the world
music backingtrack, while the
first-rate beer menu skilfully
picks its way through Belgium's
myriad beers.

Ma Rica Rokk

't Zand 6 ☎050/33 24 34. No fixed
times, but open daily from early
in the morning till late at night.
Atmospheric spot with sparse
functional decor that has long
been a local favourite with
students and townies alike.
There's a youthful clientele,
zippy service, a competent beer
menu, a summer terrace and,
at weekends, some of the best
music in town, with house
especially popular.

Wijnbar Est

Noordzandstraat 34 ☎050/33 38 39.
Mon, Thurs & Sun 5pm till late, Fri
& Sat 3pm–1am. The best wine
bar in town, with a friendly
and relaxed atmosphere, an
extensive cellar and over 25
different wines available by the
glass every day – it's especially
strong on New World vintages,
and also serves a selection of
cheeses in the evening. There's
live jazz, blues and folk music
every Sunday from 8pm to
10.30pm.

The Groeninge Museum

Recently revamped and restructured, the Groeninge Museum (Tues–Sun 9.30am–5pm; €8, including Arentshuis Museum) possesses one of the world's finest samples of early Flemish paintings, from Jan van Eyck through to Hieronymus Bosch and Jan Provoost. These paintings make up the kernel of the museum's permanent collection, but there are later (albeit lesser) pieces on display too, reaching into the twentieth century, with works by the likes of Jean Delville and Constant Permeke.

The Groeninge has just eleven rooms, chronologically arranged; the early Flemish paintings are concentrated in Rooms 1 to 3, and thereafter there are separate rooms covering periods and styles including the late Renaissance and Baroque, Neoclassicism, Expressionism and Surrealism. Room 6 is a Sculpture Hall, while Room 7 comprises five small areas with regularly rotated racks of paintings. The description below details some of the most important works and, although the collection is regularly rotated, you can expect most if not all the ones described to be on display.

Jan van Eyck

Arguably the greatest of the early Flemish masters, Jan van Eyck lived and worked in Bruges from 1430 until his death eleven years later. He was a key figure in the development of oil painting, modulating its tones to create paintings of extraordinary clarity and realism. The Groeninge has two gorgeous examples of his work in its permanent collection, beginning with the miniature portrait of his wife, *Margareta van Eyck*, painted in 1439 and bearing his motto, "als ich can" (the best I can do). The painting is very much a private picture and one that had no commercial value, marking a small step away from the sponsored art – and religious preoccupations – of previous Flemish artists.

The second Eyck painting is the remarkable *Madonna and Child with Canon George van der Paele*, a glowing and richly symbolic work with three figures surrounding the Madonna: the kneeling canon, St George (his patron saint) and St Donatian, to whom he is being presented. St George doffs his helmet to salute the infant Christ and speaks by means of the Hebrew word *Adonai* (Lord)

▲ MARGARETA VAN EYCK, JAN VAN EYCK

> Jan van Eyck's most magnificent painting, the extraordinary *Adoration of the Mystic Lamb*, is displayed in St Baafskathedraal in Ghent (see p.115).

inscribed on his chin strap, while Jesus replies through the green parrot in his left hand: folklore asserted that this type of parrot was fond of saying "Ave", the Latin for "welcome". The canon's face is exquisitely executed, down to the sagging jowls and the bulging blood vessels at his temple, while the glasses and book in his hand add to his air of deep contemplation. Audaciously, van Eyck has broken with tradition by painting the canon amongst the saints rather than as a lesser figure – a distinct nod to the humanism that was gathering pace in contemporary Bruges. The painting also celebrates the wealth of Bruges in the luxurious clothes and furnishings: the floor tiles are of Spanish design, the geometric tapestry at the feet of the Madonna comes from Asia and St Donatian is decked out in jewel-encrusted vestments.

Rogier van der Weyden and Hugo van der Goes

The Groeninge possesses two fine and roughly contemporaneous copies of paintings by Rogier van der Weyden (1399–1464), one-time official city painter to Brussels. The first is a tiny *Portrait of Philip the Good*, in which the pallor of the duke's aquiline features, along with the brightness of his hatpin and chain of office, are skilfully balanced by the sombre cloak and hat. The second and much larger painting, *St Luke Painting the Portrait of Our Lady*, is a rendering of a popular if highly improbable legend which claimed that Luke painted Mary – thereby becoming the patron saint of painters. The painting is notable for the detail of its Flemish background and the cheeky-chappie smile of the baby Christ.

One the most gifted of the early Flemish artists, Hugo van der Goes (died 1482) is a shadowy figure, though it is known that he became master of the painters' guild in Ghent in 1467. Eight years later, he entered a Ghent priory as a lay brother, perhaps related to the prolonged bouts of acute depression which afflicted him. Few of his paintings have survived, but these exhibit a superb compositional balance and a keen observational eye. His last work, the luminescent *Death of Our Lady*, is here at the Groeninge, though it was originally hung in the abbey at Koksijde on the coast. Sticking to religious legend, the Apostles have been miraculously transported to Mary's

▲ *DEATH OF OUR LADY*, VAN DER GOES

▲ *TRIPTYCH OF WILLEM MOREEL*, MEMLING

deathbed, where, in a state of agitation, they surround the prostrate woman. Mary is dressed in blue, but there are no signs of luxury, reflecting both der Goes' asceticism and his polemic – the artist may well have been appalled by the church's love of glitter and gold.

The Master of the St Ursula Legend

Another Groeninge highlight is the two matching panels of *The Legend of St Ursula*, the work of an unknown fifteenth-century artist known as the Master of the St Ursula Legend. The panels, each of which displays five miniature scenes, were probably inspired by the twelfth-century discovery of the supposed bones of St Ursula and the women who were massacred with her in Cologne seven centuries before – a sensational find that would certainly have been common knowledge in Bruges. Surfacing in the ninth century, the original legend describes St Ursula as a British princess who avoids an unwanted marriage by going on a pilgrimage to Rome accompanied by eleven female companions, sometimes referred to as nuns or virgins. On their way back, a tempest blows their ship off course and they land at Cologne, where the (pagan) Huns promptly slaughter them.

Pious women who suffered for the faith always went down a storm in medieval Christendom, but somewhere along the line the eleven women became eleven thousand – possibly because the buckets of bones found in Cologne were from an old public burial ground and had nothing to do with Ursula and her chums.

Hans Memling

The work of Hans Memling (1430–1494) is represented by a pair of *Annunciation* panels from a triptych – gentle, romantic representations of an angel and Mary in contrasting shades of grey, a monochrome technique known as *grisaille*. Here also is Memling's *Moreel Triptych*, in which the formality of the design is offset by the warm colours and the gentleness of the detail – St Giles strokes the fawn and the knight's hand lies on the donor's shoulder. The central panel depicts saints Giles and Maurus to either side of St Christopher with a backdrop of mountains, clouds and sea. St Christopher, the patron saint of travellers, carries Jesus on his shoulders in an abbreviated reference to the original story which has the saint, who made his living lugging travellers across a river, carrying a child who becomes impossibly heavy. In the way of such things,

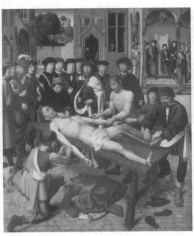

▲ JUDGEMENT OF CAMBYSES, DAVID

with the *Baptism of Christ Triptych*, in which a boyish, lightly bearded Christ is depicted as part of the Holy Trinity in the central panel. To either side are the donors, the Trompes, and their patron saints – St John and St Elizabeth. There's also one of David's few secular ventures in the Groeninge, the intriguing *Judgement of Cambyses*, painted on two oak panels. Based on a Persian legend related by Herodotus, the first panel's background shows the corrupt judge Sisamnes accepting a bribe, with the result, while his arrest by grim-faced aldermen fills the rest of the panel. The aldermen crowd in on Sisamnes with a palpable sense of menace and, as the king sentences him to be flayed alive, a sweaty look of fear sweeps over the judge's face. In the gruesome second panel the king's servants carry out the judgement, applying themselves to the task with clinical detachment. Behind, in the top-right corner, the fable is completed with the judge's son dispensing justice from his father's old chair, which is now draped with the flayed skin. Completed in 1498, the painting was hung in the council chamber by the city burghers to encourage honesty amongst its magistrates and as a sort of public apology for the imprisonment of Archduke Maximilian in Bruges in 1488. Maximilian would almost certainly have appreciated the painting – even if the gesture was itself too little, too late

it turns out that the child is Jesus and the realization turns Christopher Christian. The side-panels show the donors and their sixteen children along with their patron saints – the knight St William for Willem Moreel, a wealthy spice trader and financier, and St Barbara for his wife.

There's more work by this artist on display at the Memling Collection (see p.73).

Gerard David and Hieronymus Bosch

Born near Gouda, the Dutchman Gerard David (c.1460–1523) moved to Bruges in his early twenties. Soon admitted into the local painters' guild, he quickly rose through the ranks, becoming the city's leading artistic light after the death of Memling. Official commissions rained in on David, mostly for religious paintings, which he approached in a formal manner but with a fine eye for detail. The Groeninge holds two excellent examples of his work, starting

– as the king dispenses his judgement without reference to either the Church or God, a sub-text of secular authority very much to his tastes.

The Groeninge also holds Hieronymus Bosch's (1450–1516) *Last Judgement*, a trio of oak panels crammed with mysterious beasts, microscopic mutants and scenes of awful cruelty – men boiled in a pit or cut in half by a giant knife. It looks like unbridled fantasy, but in fact the scenes were read as symbols, a sort of strip cartoon of legend, proverb and tradition. Indeed Bosch's religious orthodoxy is confirmed by the appeal his work had for that most Catholic of Spanish kings, Philip II.

Jan Provoost and Adriaen Isenbrant

There's more grim symbolism in Jan Provoost's (1465–1529) crowded and melodramatic *Last Judgement*, painted for the Stadhuis in 1525, and his striking *The Miser and Death*, which portrays the merchant with his money in one panel, trying desperately to pass a promissory note to the grinning skeleton in the next. Provoost's career was typical of many of the Flemish artists of the early sixteenth century. Initially he worked in the Flemish manner, his style greatly influenced by Gerard David, but from about 1521 his work was reinvigorated by contact with the German painter and engraver Albrecht Dürer, who had himself been inspired by the artists of the early Italian Renaissance. Provoost moved around too, working in Valenciennes and Antwerp, before settling in Bruges in 1494. One of his Bruges contemporaries was Adriaen Isenbrant (died 1551), whose speciality was small, precisely executed panels. His *Virgin and Child* triptych is a good example of his technically proficient work.

Bernard van Orley

Bernard van Orley (1488–1541) was a long-time favourite of the Habsburg officials in Brussels

▲ *LAST JUDGEMENT*, BOSCH

until his Protestant sympathies put him in the commercial doghouse. A versatile artist, Orley produced action-packed paintings of biblical scenes, often backdropped by classical buildings in the Renaissance style, as well as cartoon designs for tapestries, sometimes for the creation of stained-glass windows. He is represented in the Groeninge collection by the strip-cartoon *Legend of St Rochus*. A fourteenth-century saint hailing from Montpellier in France, Rochus was in northern Italy on a pilgrimage to Rome when the plague struck. He abandoned his journey to tend to the sick and promptly discovered he had miraculous healing powers. This did not stop him from catching the plague himself, but fortunately a remarkable dog was on hand to nurse him back to health. Recovered, Rochus went back home, but his relatives failed to recognize him and he was imprisoned as an impostor, and died there – a hard luck story if ever there was one.

Pieter Pourbus, Frans the Elder and Frans the Younger

The Groeninge's collection of late sixteenth- and seventeenth-century paintings isn't especially strong, but there's enough to discern the period's watering-down of religious themes in favour of more secular preoccupations. Pieter Pourbus (1523–1584) is well represented by a series of austere and often surprisingly unflattering portraits of the movers and shakers of his day. There's also his *Last Judgement*, a much larger but atypical work, crammed with muscular men and fleshy women; completed in 1551, its inspiration came from Michelangelo's Sistine Chapel. Born in Gouda, Pourbus moved to Bruges in his early twenties, becoming the leading local portraitist of his day as well as squeezing in work as a civil engineer and cartographer. Pieter was the first of an artistic dynasty with his son, Frans the Elder (1545–1581), jumping municipal ship to move to Antwerp as Bruges slipped into

the economic doldrums. Frans was a noted portraitist too, but his success was trifling in comparison with that of his son, Frans the Younger (1569–1622), who became one of Europe's most celebrated portraitists, working for the Habsburgs and the Medicis amongst a bevy of powerful families. In the permanent collection is a fine example of his work, an exquisite double portrait of the *Archdukes Albert and Isabella*.

Jacob van Oost the Elder

Jacob van Oost the Elder (1603–1671) was the city's most prominent artist during the Baroque period and the Groeninge has a substantial sample of his work. However, his canvases are pretty meagre stuff (and are often not displayed at all). His *Portrait of a Theologian*, for example, is a stultifyingly formal and didactic affair only partly redeemed by its crisp draughtsmanship, while his *Portrait of a Bruges Family* drips with bourgeois sentimentality.

The Symbolists

The Groeninge has a substantial collection of nineteenth- and early twentieth-century Belgian art, but not nearly enough gallery space to display it all – in Rooms 5 to 11. Consequently, even the more significant paintings aren't always on display. There are, however, certain obvious highlights, beginning with the Symbolists, amongst whom Jean Delville (1867–1953) takes pride of place with his enormous (and inordinately weird) *De Godmens* – a repulsive, yet compelling picture of writhing bodies yearning for salvation. Delville was an ardent and prolific polemicist for modern art, constantly redefining its aesthetic as he himself changed his style and technique. This particular piece, from 1903, was arguably the high point of his Symbolist period and accorded with his assertion, in *La Mission de L'Art*, that art should have a messianic ideal and a redemptive quality.

Delville's contemporary – and fellow Symbolist – Fernand Khnopff (1858–1921) is represented by *Secret Reflections*, not one of his better paintings perhaps, but interesting in so far as its lower panel, showing the St Janshospitaal (see p.72) reflected in a canal, confirms one of the Symbolists' favourite conceits: "Bruges the dead city". This was inspired by Georges Rodenbach's novel *Bruges la Morte*, a highly stylized muse on love and obsession first published in 1892, and the book which kick-started the craze for visiting Bruges, the "dead city", where the action unfolds. The upper panel of Khnopff's painting is a play on appearance and desire, but it's pretty feeble, unlike his later attempts, in which he painted his sister, Marguerite, again and again, using her refined, almost plastic beauty to stir a vague sense of passion – for she's desirable and utterly unobtainable in equal measure.

The Expressionists and Surrealists

The Groeninge has a healthy sample of the work of the talented Constant Permeke (1886–1952). Wounded in World War I, Permeke's grim wartime experiences helped him develop a distinctive Expressionist style in which his subjects – usually agricultural workers, fishermen and so

▲ SERENITY, DELVAUX

Woestijne (1881–1947), another excellent example of Belgian Expressionism, with Jesus and the disciples, all elliptical eyes and restrained movement, trapped within prison-like walls.

Also noteworthy is the spookily stark surrealism of Paul Delvaux's (1897–1994) *Serenity*. One of the most interesting of Belgium's modern artists, Delvaux started out as an Expressionist but came to – and stayed with – Surrealism in the 1930s. Two of his pet motifs were train stations, in one guise or another, and nude or semi-nude women set against some sort of classical backdrop. The intention was to usher the viewer into the unconscious with dreamlike images where every perspective was exact, and there is indeed something very unsettling about his vision, largely because of the impeccable craftsmanship. At their best, his paintings achieve an almost palpable sense of foreboding – and *Serenity* is a first-class example.

forth – were monumental in form, but invested with sombre, sometimes threatening emotion. His charcoal drawing the *Angelus* is a typically dark and earthy representation of Belgian peasant life dated 1934. In similar vein is the enormous *Last Supper* by Gustave van de

The Groeninge also owns a couple of minor oils and a number of etchings and drawings by James Ensor (1860–1949), one of Belgium's most innovative painters, and Magritte's (1898–1967) characteristically unnerving *The Assault*.

North and east of the Markt

The gentle canals and maze-like cobbled streets of eastern Bruges are extraordinarily pretty, and it's here that the city reveals its depth of character. In this uncrowded part of the centre, which stretches east from Jan van Eyckplein to the old medieval moat, several different types of architecture blend into an almost seamless whole, beginning with the classically picturesque terraces that date from the town's late medieval golden age. The most characteristic architectural feature is the crow-step gable, popular from the fourteenth to the eighteenth century and revived by the restorers of the 1880s and later, but there are also expansive classical mansions and humble cottages. Almost always the buildings are of brick, reflecting the shortage of local stone and the abundance of polder peat, which was used to fire clay bricks, clay being another common commodity hereabouts. Above all, eastern Bruges excels in its detail, surprising the eye again and again with its subtle variety, featuring everything from intimate arched doorways, bendy tiled roofs and wonky chimneys through to a bevy of discreet shrines and miniature statues.

Nevertheless, there are one or two obvious targets for the visitor, beginning with the Kantcentrum (Lace Centre), where you can buy locally made lace and watch its manufacture, and the city's most unusual church, the adjacent Jeruzalemkerk. In addition, the Folklore Museum holds a passably interesting collection of local bygones, while the Museum Onze-Lieve-Vrouw ter Potterie (Museum of Our Lady of the Pottery) has an intriguing chapel and several fine Flemish tapestries.

St Jakobskerk

Sint Jakobsstraat. April–Sept Mon–Sat 10am–noon & 2–5pm, Sun 2–5pm;

free. St Jakobskerk's sombre exterior, mostly dating from the fifteenth century, clusters round a chunky tower. In medieval times the church was popular with the foreign merchants who had congregated in Bruges, acting as a sort of prototype community centre; it also marked the western limit of the foreign merchants' quarter. Inside, the church is mainly Baroque, its airy nave leading to a massive high altar. It also possesses the handsome early Renaissance burial chapel of Ferry de Gros (died 1547), to the right of the choir, which sports the elaborate, painted tomb of this well-to-do landowner. Unusually, the tomb has two shelves – on the top are the finely carved effigies of Ferry and his first wife, while below, on the lower shelf, is his second. Here also, above the altar, is an enamelled terracotta medallion of the Virgin and Child imported from Florence some time in the fifteenth century. No one knows quite how it ended up here, but there's no doubt that it influenced Flemish artists of the period – in the same way as Michelangelo's statue in the Onze Lieve Vrouwekerk (see p.70). The walls of St Jakobskerk are covered with around eighty paintings bequeathed by the city's merchants. They're not an especially distinguished bunch, but look out for the finely executed *Legend of St Lucy*, a panel triptych by the Master of the St Lucy Legend that tracks through the sufferings of this fourth-century saint in some detail; it's located in St Anthony's Chapel – the first chapel on the left-hand side of the nave. In the next chapel along, look out for the meditative *Madonna and the Seven Sorrows*, a triptych by Pieter Pourbus (1523–1584), the leading local artist of his

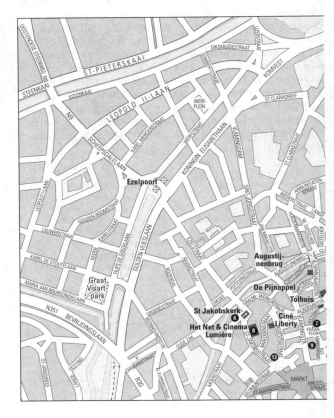

day. St Jakobskerk also has a first-rate assortment of brass funeral plaques, though putative brassrubbers will need to bring their own gear.

Kraanplein

East of St Jakobskerk lies Kraanplein – Crane Square – whose name recalls one of the medieval city's main attractions, the enormous wooden crane that once unloaded heavy goods from the adjoining river. Before it was covered over, the River Reie ran south from Jan van Eyckplein to the Markt, and the Kraanplein dock was

one of the busiest parts of this central waterway. Mounted on a revolving post in the manner of a windmill, the crane's pulleys were worked by means of two large treadmills operated by children – a grim existence by any measure. Installed in 1290 – and only dismantled in 1767 – the crane impressed visitors greatly and was as sure a sign of Bruges' economic success as the Belfort. The crane crops up in the background of several medieval paintings, notably behind St John in Memling's *Mystical Marriage of St Catherine* (see p.74).

PLACES North and east of the Markt

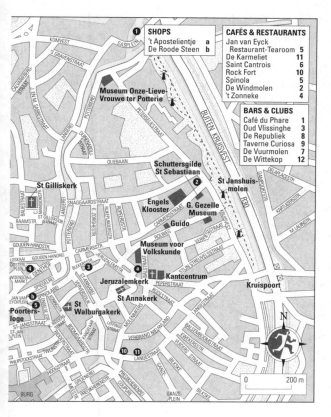

▲ JAN VAN EYCKPLEIN

PLACES

North and east of the Markt

Jan van Eyckplein

North of Kraanplein lies Jan van Eyckplein, one of the prettiest squares in Bruges, its cobbles backdropped by the easy sweep of the Spiegelrei canal. The centrepiece of the square is an earnest statue of van Eyck, erected in 1878, whilst on the north side is the Tolhuis, whose fancy Renaissance entrance is decorated with the coat of arms of the dukes of Luxembourg, who long levied tolls here. The Tolhuis dates from the late fifteenth century, but was extensively remodelled in medieval style in the 1870s, as was the Poortersloge (Merchants' Lodge), whose slender tower pokes up above the rooftops on the west side of the square. Theoretically, any city merchant was entitled to be a member of the Poortersloge, but in fact membership was restricted to the richest and the most powerful. An informal alternative to the Town Hall, it was here that key political and economic decisions were taken and it was also where local bigwigs could drink and gamble discreetly.

The Spiegelrei canal and the Augustijnenbrug

Running east from Jan van Eyckplein, the Spiegelrei canal was once the heart of the foreign merchants' quarter, its frenetic quays overlooked by the trade missions of many of the city's trading partners. The medieval buildings were demolished long ago but have been replaced by an exquisite medley of architectural styles from expansive Georgian mansions to pirouetting crow-step gables.

At the far end of Spiegelrei, turn left onto Gouden-Handrei, which, along with adjoining Spaanse Loskaai, flanks an especially attractive sliver of canal that was once used as a quay by Bruges' Spanish merchants. On the far side of the canal stand a string of delightful summer outhouses, privately owned and sometimes surprisingly lavish extensions to the demure houses fronting onto Gouden-Handstraat.

At the west end of Spaanse Loskaai is the Augustijnenbrug, the city's oldest surviving bridge, a sturdy three-arched structure dating from 1391. The bridge was built to help the monks of a nearby (and long-demolished)

Augustinian monastery get into the city centre speedily; the benches set into the parapet were cut to allow itinerant tradesmen to display their goods here.

Running south from the bridge is Spanjaardstraat, which was also part of the Spanish enclave. It was here, at no.9, in a house formerly known as De Pijnappel (The Fir Cone), that the founder of the Jesuits, Ignatius Loyola (1491–1556), spent his holidays while he was a student in Paris. He befriended Juan Luis Vives (see p.68), who lodged down the street, but unfortunately his friend's liberality failed to temper Loyola's nascent fanaticism. Spanjaardstraat leads back to Jan van Eyckplein.

St Gilliskerk

St Gilliskerkhof. April–Sept Mon–Sat 10am–noon & 2–5pm, Sun 2–5pm; free. The sturdy brick pile of St Gilliskerk dates from the late thirteenth century, but was greatly enlarged in the 1460s; the church has a wide and appealing three-aisled nave, but its most distinctive feature is the unusual barrel-vaulted roof added in the eighteenth century. Among the paintings on display, the pick is the Hemelsdale polyptych by the prolific Pieter Pourbus (on the wall just to the right of the main doors). It's a dainty piece of work with the donors

at either end sandwiching three scenes from the life of Christ – the Adoration of the Shepherds, the Flight into Egypt and Jesus's Circumcision. The church also possesses a set of six eighteenth-century paintings illustrating the efforts of the Trinitarian monks to ransom Christian prisoners from the Turks. In themselves, the paintings are distinctly second-rate, but the two near the organ in the top right-hand corner of the church are interesting in their sinister representation of the east – all glowering clouds and gloomy city walls. The other four paintings, in the bottom left-hand corner of the nave, explain the papal foundation, in 1198, of the Trinitarians, an order specifically devoted to the ransom of Christians held by Muslims, and one which enjoyed strong support from St Gilliskerk.

▲ SPIEGELREI CANAL

St Walburgakerk

Koningstraat. April–Sept Mon–Sat 10am–noon & 2–5pm, Sun 2–5pm; free. Southeast of Jan van Eyckplein, St Walburgakerk is a fluent Baroque extravagance built for the Jesuits in the first half of the seventeenth century. Decorated with podgy cherubs and slender pilasters, the sinuous, flowing facade is matched by the extravagance of the booming interior, awash with acres of creamy-white paint. The grandiose pulpit is the work of Artus II Quellin (1625–1700), an Antwerp woodcarver and sculptor whose family ran a profitable sideline in Baroque pulpits; there are more of his huffing and puffing cherubs on the main altarpieces.

The pick of the church's scattering of paintings is a Pieter Claeissens triptych – on the right-hand side of the nave. The central panel depicts a popular

▲ KANTCENTRUM, PIECES OF LACE

legend relating to Philip the Good, a fifteenth-century count of Flanders and the founder of the Order of the Golden Fleece (see p.75). The story goes that, while Philip was preparing to fight the French, he encountered the Virgin Mary in a scorched tree; not one to look a gift horse in the mouth, Philip fell to his knees and asked for victory, and his prayers were promptly answered.

St Annakerk

April–Sept Mon–Sat 10am–noon & 2–5pm, Sun 2–5pm; free. The original Gothic St Annakerk was burnt to the ground in the religious wars of the sixteenth century and today's dinky little structure, complete with the slenderest of brick towers, is a notably homogeneous example of the Baroque, with pride of interior place going to the marble and porphyry rood screen of 1628.

The Kantcentrum

Peperstraat 3. Mon–Fri 10am–noon & 2–6pm, Sat 10am–noon & 2–5pm; €2.50. Just east of St Annakerk is an old working-class district of low brick cottages. In the middle of this district, at the foot of Balstraat, lies a complex of buildings which originally belonged to the wealthy Adornes family, who migrated here from Genoa in

▲ ST WALBURGAKERK

the thirteenth century. Inside the complex, the Kantcentrum (Lace Centre), on the right-hand side of the entrance, has a couple of busy workshops and offers very informal demonstrations of traditional lacemaking in the afternoon (no set times). They sell the stuff, too – both here and in the shop at the ticket kiosk – but it isn't cheap: a smallish Bruges table mat, with two swans, for example, costs €80; if you fancy having a go yourself, the shop has all the gubbins.

The Jeruzalemkerk

Peperstraat. Same times and ticket as the Kantcentrum (see opposite). Across the passageway is one of the city's real oddities, the Jeruzalemkerk. This was built by the Adornes family in the fifteenth century as an approximate copy of the Church of the Holy Sepulchre in Jerusalem after one of their number, Pieter, had returned from a pilgrimage to the Holy Land. The interior is on two levels: the lower one is dominated by a large and ghoulish altarpiece, decorated with skulls and ladders, in front of which is the black marble tomb of Anselm Adornes, the son of the church's founder, and his wife Margaretha. The pilgrimage didn't bring the Adornes family much luck: Anselm was murdered in gruesome circumstances in Scotland in 1483 while serving as Bruges' consul. There's more grisliness at the back of the church, where the small vaulted chapel holds a replica of Christ's tomb – you can glimpse the imitation body down the tunnel behind the iron grating. To either side of the main altar, steps ascend to the choir, which is situated right below the eccentric, onion-domed lantern tower.

Lace Museum

Behind the Jeruzalemkerk, the tiny Lace Museum (Kantmuseum; same times and ticket as the church) is of passing interest for its samples of antique lace. Renowned for the fineness of its thread and beautiful motifs, Belgian lace – or Flanders lace as it was formerly known – is famous the world over. It was once worn in the courts of Brussels, Paris, Madrid and London – Queen Elizabeth I of England is said to have had no fewer than three thousand lace dresses – and Bruges was a centre of its production. Handmade lace reached the peak of its popularity in the early nineteenth century, when hundreds of Bruges women and girls worked as home-based

▼ JERUZALEMKERK

PLACES North and east of the Markt

lacemakers. The industry was, however, transformed by the arrival of machine-made lace in the 1840s and, by the end of the century, handmade lace had been largely supplanted by the lacemakers obliged to work in factories. This highly mechanized industry collapsed after World War I, when lace, a symbol of an old and discredited order, suddenly had no place in the wardrobe of most women.

The Lace Museum holds fifty-odd examples of old, handmade lace, the most elaborate of which is its sample of late nineteenth-century Chantilly lace. Incidentally, most lace shops in Bruges – and there are lots – sell lace manufactured in the Far East, especially China. The best lace shop in town – for locally made lace – is 't Apostelientje (see p.104), very close to the Kantcentrum at Balstraat 11.

Museum voor Volkskunde

Balstraat. Tues–Sun 9.30am–5pm; €3. At the north end of Balstraat, the Museum voor Volkskunde (Folklore Museum) occupies a long line of low-ceilinged almshouses set beside a trim courtyard. It's a varied collection, with the emphasis on the nineteenth and early twentieth centuries, but the labelling is patchy so it's best to pick up an English guidebook at reception. Rooms 1–5 are to the right of the entrance, rooms 6–14 are dead ahead. Beside the entrance, in Room 15, *De Zwarte Kat* – the Black Cat – is a small tavern done out in traditional style and serving ales and snacks.

The string of period shops and workshops includes a confectioner's shop, in room 2, where in summer there are occasional demonstrations of traditional sweet-making. Next door, in Room 3, is an intriguing assortment of biscuit and chocolate moulds as well as cake decorations (*patacons*). Made of clay, these *patacons* were painted by hand in true folksy style, with the three most popular motifs being animals, military scenes and Bible stories.

▲ FOLKLORE MUSEUM

Moving on, Room 6 holds a modest but enjoyable display of local costumes and textiles, including several samplers made by trainee lacemakers, and Room 7 is a re-created classroom from circa 1920. Room 11 focuses on popular religion, with an interesting collection of pilgrimage banners plus the wax, silver and iron *ex votos* that still hang in many Flemish churches. Traditionally, the believer makes a promise to God – say, to behave better – and then asks for a blessing, like the curing of a bad leg. Sometimes the *ex voto* is hung up once the promise is made, but mostly it's done afterwards, in gratitude for the cure or blessing.

Rooms 13 and 14 hold a diverting display on pipes and tobacco. There are all sorts of antique smokers' paraphernalia – tobacco cutters, lighters, tinder boxes and so forth – but it's the selection of pipes which catches the eye, especially the long, thin ones made of clay. Clay pipes were notoriously brittle, so smokers invested in pipe cases, of which several are exhibited.

The Guido Gezelle Museum

Rolweg 64. Tues–Sun 9.30am–12.30pm & 1.30–5pm; €2. The Guido Gezelle Museum commemorates the poet-priest Guido Gezelle (1830–1899), a leading figure in nineteenth-century Bruges. Gezelle was born in this substantial brick cottage, which now contains a few knick-knacks such as Gezelle's old chair and pipes, plus his death mask, though it's mostly devoted to a biographical account of his life. The labelling is, however, only in Dutch and you really need to be a Gezelle enthusiast to get much out of it. Neither is Gezelle to everyone's

▲ GUIDO GEZELLE MUSEUM

tastes. His poetry is pretty average and the fact that he translated Longfellow's *Song of Hiawatha* into Dutch is the sort of detail that bores rather than inspires.

More importantly, Gezelle played a key role in the preservation of many of the city's medieval buildings and was instrumental in the creation of the Gruuthuse Museum (see p.69). Gezelle believed that the survival of the medieval city symbolized the continuity of the Catholic faith, a mind-set similar to that of the city's Flemish nationalists, who resisted change and championed medieval – or at least neo-Gothic – architecture to maintain Flemish "purity". Gezelle resisted cultural change, too: a secular theatre appalled him, prompting him to write: "We are smothered by displays of adultery and incest… and the foundations of the family and of marriage are [being] undermined".

▲ ST JANSHUISMOLEN WINDMILL

St Janshuismolen and the Kruispoort

At the east end of Rolweg, a long and wide earthen bank marks the path of the old town walls. Perched on top are a quartet of windmills – two clearly visible close by and another two beyond eyeshot, about 300m and 500m to the north. You'd have to be something of a windmill fanatic to want to visit them all, but the nearest two are mildly diverting – and the closest, St Janshuismolen, is in working order, and the only one that is open (Tues–Sun 9.30am–12.30pm & 1.30–5pm; €2).

South of St Janshuismolen is the Kruispoort, a much-modified and strongly fortified city gate dating from 1402.

Schuttersgilde St Sebastiaan

Carmersstraat 174. Guided tours: May–Sept Tues & Wed 2–5pm, Thurs 10am–noon & 2–5pm, Fri 10am–noon, Sat 10am–noon & 2–5pm; Oct–April Wed only 2–5pm; €3. At the east end of Carmersstraat is the Schuttersgilde St Sebastiaan (The Archers' Guildhouse), a large brick guild house and tower dating from the middle of the sixteenth century. The city's archers had ceased to be of any military importance by the time of its construction, but the guild had, by then, redefined itself as an exclusive social club where the bigwigs of the day could spend their time hobnobbing. Nowadays, it's still in use as a social-cum-sports club with the archers opting either to shoot at the familiar circular targets or to plonk a replica bird on top of a pole and shoot at it from below – the traditional favourite. The escorted tour is hardly riveting, but it does include a gambol through the old dining hall, where the fireplace is surmounted by a bust of Charles II, who joined the guild when he was in exile here (see box opposite). Also included is a visit to the shooting gallery, whose medievalist stained-glass windows date from the 1950s, and a glimpse of the modern clubhouse.

The Engels Klooster

Carmersstraat 85. Wed 2–6pm, Thurs 2–4pm & Sat 10–noon; free. During

Bruges' medieval gates

Of the city's seven medieval gates, four have survived in relatively good condition, though all have been heavily restored. Apart from the Kruispoort (see above), these are the Gentpoort, on the southeast edge of the centre on Gentpoortstraat; the Smedenpoort, on the west side of the city centre at the end of Smedenstraat; and the Ezelpoort – Donkey Gate – to the northwest of the centre. All four date from the early fifteenth century and consist of twin, heavily fortified, stone walls and turrets.

Charles II in Bruges

Charles II of England, who spent three years in exile in Bruges from 1656 to 1659, was an enthusiastic member of the archers' guild and, after the Restoration, he sent them a whopping 3600 florins as a thankyou for their hospitality. Charles's enforced exile had begun in 1651 after his attempt to seize the English crown – following the Civil War and the execution of his father in 1649 – had ended in defeat by the Parliamentarians at the Battle of Worcester. Initially, Charles hightailed it to France, but Cromwell persuaded the French to expel him and the exiled king ended up seeking sanctuary in Spanish territory. He was allowed to settle in Bruges, then part of the Spanish Netherlands, though the Habsburgs were stingy when it came to granting Charles and his retinue an allowance. The royalists were, says a courtier's letter of 1657, "never in greater want... for Englishmen cannot live on bread alone". In addition, Cromwell's spies kept an eagle eye on Charles's activities, filing lurid reports about his conduct. A certain Mr Butler informed Cromwell that "I think I may truly say that greater abominations were never practised among people than at Charles Stuart's court. Fornication, drunkenness and adultery are considered no sins amongst them." It must have made Cromwell's hair stand on end. Cromwell died in 1658 and Charles was informed of this whilst he was playing tennis in Bruges. The message was to the point – "The devil is dead" – and Charles was on the English throne two years later.

his stay in Bruges, the exiled king Charles II worshipped at the Engels Klooster (English Convent) on Carmersstraat 85. Founded in 1629, the convent was long a haven for English Catholic exiles, though this didn't stop Queen Victoria from popping in during her visit to Belgium in 1843. Nowadays, the convent's nuns provide an enthusiastic twenty-minute guided tour of the lavishly decorated Baroque church, whose finest features are the handsome cupola and the altar, an extraordinarily flashy affair made of 23 different types of marble. It was the gift of the Nithsdales, English aristocrats whose loyalty to the Catholic faith got them into no end of scrapes.

Museum Onze-Lieve-Vrouw ter Potterie

Potterierei 79; Tues–Sun 9.30am– 12.30pm & 1.30–5pm; €2.50. The Museum Onze-Lieve-Vrouw ter Potterie (Museum of Our Lady of the Pottery) was founded as a hospital in the thirteenth century on the site of an earlier pottery – hence the name. The hospital (though "hospital" is a tad misleading, as the buildings were originally used as much to accommodate visitors as tend the sick) was remodelled on several occasions and the three brick gables that front the building today span three

▲ ENGELS KLOOSTER

centuries. The middle gable is the oldest, dating from 1359 and built as part of the first hospital chapel. The left-hand gable belonged to the main medieval hospital ward and the one on the right marks a second chapel, added in the 1620s.

Inside, a visit to the museum begins in the former sick room, where a distinctly mediocre selection of medieval religious paintings is partly redeemed by an arresting panel-painting of *St Michael* triumphing over the devil, by the Master of the St Ursula Legend. Moving on, the museum's chapel is an L-shaped affair distinguished by a sumptuous marble rood screen, whose two side altars recall the museum's location beside what was once one of the city's busiest quays. The altar on the left is dedicated to St Anthony, the patron saint of ships' joiners, the one on the right to St Brendan, the patron saint of seamen. There's also a finely expressed thirteenth-century stone statue of the Virgin on the main altar, but pride of place goes to the set of old tapestries that are hung in the chapel from Easter to October. These comprise a superbly naturalistic, brightly coloured strip cartoon depicting eighteen miracles attributed to Our Lady of the Pottery, almost all to do with being saved from the sea or a sudden change of fortune in fishing or trade. Each carries an inscription, but you'll need to be good at Dutch to decipher them.

Shops

't Apostelientje
Balstraat 11 ☏ 050/33 78 60. Mon–Fri 9.30am–6pm, Sat 9.30am–5pm, Sun 10am–1pm. Close to the Kantcentrum, this small shop sells a charming variety of handmade lace pieces of both modern and traditional design. If there's nothing here that takes your fancy, then try the (even smaller) shop in the Kantcentrum itself.

De Roode Steen
Jan van Eyckplein 8 ☏ 050/33 61 51. Mon, Tues, Thurs & Fri 10.30am–6.30pm, Sat & Sun 1–6.30pm. Occupying a splendid fifteenth-century house across from the Tolhuis, this shop specializes in

▲ DE WINDMOLEN

interior design, with heaps of sumptuous soft furnishings and well-made furniture, as well as smaller items like cushions and lamps.

Cafés and restaurants

Jan van Eyck Tearoom
Jan van Eyckplein 12 ☎050/61 01 01. Daily except Wed 10am–10pm. Set in an agreeable location beside one of the city's prettier squares, this neat and cheerily decorated little café-cum-tearoom serves up tasty snacks and light meals, with friendly service and affordable prices, plus thirteen sorts of beer. Main courses work out at about €15–18, veggie dishes at around €10. There's also a pavement terrace.

De Karmeliet
Langestraat 19 ☎050/33 82 59. Tues 7–9.30pm, Wed–Sat noon–2pm & 7–9.30pm, Sun noon–2pm. Smooth and polished restaurant – one of the city's best – occupying a big, old mansion about five minutes' walk east of the Burg. It's a tad formal for many tastes, but there's no disputing the excellence of the service or the quality of the French cuisine. The inventive menu features dishes like rabbit (*lapin royale*) and marinated cod. Set menus (from €45) plus à la carte (main from around €40). Reservations essential.

Rock Fort
Langestraat 15 ☎050/33 41 13. Mon, Tues & Thurs–Sat noon–2.30pm & 6–11pm, Sun 6–11pm. Smart little family-owned café-bistro serving up tasty salads, pastas and seafood. Main courses average around €18.

Saint Cantrois
Sint Jakobsstraat 53 ☎050/67 00 99, ⓦwww.saintcantrois.be. Daily except Wed 11.30am–2.30pm & 6.30–11pm. This elegant restaurant features French cuisine – and French background music – and attracts a stylish clientele. Dishes include lobster bouillabaisse and duck served in a caramelized apple sauce (from around €24). The bar is open till 3am, and there's a small garden terrace too.

Spinola
Spinolarei 1 ☎050/34 17 85. Tues–Sat noon–1.30pm & 7–9pm, Mon & Sun 7–9pm. Immaculate restaurant in a beautiful old building overlooking Jan van Eyckplein. The lively modern menu features unusual sauces and prime delicacies, from eel and veal to the freshest of seafood. The sole fillet is particularly tasty, as are the steaks. Everything is freshly prepared and there's some waiting involved – so sit back and relax. Main courses €25–35.

De Windmolen
Carmersstraat 135 ☎050/33 97 39. Mon–Thurs 10am–10pm, Fri & Sun 10am–3pm. This amiable, neighbourhood joint in an old brick house at the east end of Carmersstraat dishes up a decent line in inexpensive snacks and light meals – croque monsieur, spaghetti, lasagne and so forth – and has a competent beer menu. There's a pleasant outside terrace and the interior is dotted with folksy knick-knacks, especially ceramic windmills – appropriately, given both the name of the place and its proximity to a quartet of old windmills (see p.102).

In Den Wittekop

St Jakobsstraat 14 ☎050/33 20 59.
Tues–Sat noon–2pm & 6–10pm. This
small and intimate restaurant
is one of the most appealing
in town, its decor a fetching
mixture of the tasteful and the
kitsch. There's smooth jazz and
blues background music plus
good Flemish food, including
the local speciality of pork and
beef stewed in Trappist beer.
Mains around €17.

't Zonneke

Genthof 5 ☎050/33 07 81. Tues–Sat
12.30–2pm & 6.30–10pm, Sun 12.30–
2pm. Cosy restaurant whose
modern decor incorporates a
few of the premises' original
sixteenth-century features. The
friendly staff serve well-cooked
meals such as steak and pasta,
as well as an ample selection of
fish dishes, from around €18.

Bars and clubs

Café du Phare

Sasplein 2 ☎050/34 35 90, ⓦwww
.duphare.be. Daily except Tues 11am
till late. Off the beaten track in
the northeast corner of the
city centre, this busy place
offers filling food, a good range
of beers and a canal setting.
There's also a pleasant summer
terrace and evening jazz and
blues concerts every month or
so – come early to get a seat.
Incidentally, the odd wooden
structure across the canal is a
replica of Bruges' famous old
crane – for more on which, see
p.95.

Oud Vlissinghe

Blekersstraat 2 ☎050/34 37 37,
ⓦwww.cafevlissinghe.be. Wed–Sat
11am–midnight, Sun 11am–7pm.
With its wood panelling, antique
paintings and long wooden tables,
this is one of the oldest and
most distinctive bars in Bruges,
thought to date from 1515. The
atmosphere is relaxed and easy-
going, with the emphasis on
quiet conversation – there are no
jukeboxes here. There's a pleasant
garden terrace, too.

De Republiek

Sint Jacobsstraat 36 ☎050/34 02 29.
Daily 11am till 3/4am. One of the
most fashionable and popular
café-bars in town – though not
necessarily the most welcoming
staff – with an arty, sometimes
alternative crew. Also does
very reasonably priced snacks,
including vegetarian food and
pasta.

Taverne Curiosa

Vlamingstraat 22 ☎050/34 23
34. Tues–Sat 11am–1am, Sun
noon–midnight. Occupying an old
vaulted cellar, this popular bar-
restaurant has a good beer list
of around sixty different brews
and also offers filling snacks
and meals at reasonable prices
(mains around €13), but is best
as a bar.

De Vuurmolen

Kraanplein 5 ☎050/33 00 79, ⓦwww.
vuurmolen.com. Daily 10am–7am.
This crowded, youthful bar has a
reasonably wide range of beers,
a large front terrace and some
of the best DJs in town playing
a good mix of sounds – techno
through house and beyond.

Damme

Now a popular day-trippers' destination, well-known for its easy-going atmosphere and clutch of classy restaurants, the quaint village of Damme, 7km northeast of Bruges, was in medieval times the town's main seaport. At its height, it boasted a population of ten thousand and guarded the banks of the River Zwin, which gave Bruges direct access to the sea. The river silted up in the late fifteenth century, however, and Damme slipped into a long decline, its old brick buildings rusting away until the tourists and second-homers arrived to create the pretty and genteel village of today.

Damme's one main street, Kerkstraat, is edged by what remains of the medieval town, most memorably the Stadhuis (Town Hall) and the Onze Lieve Vrouwekerk (Church of Our Lady). Kerkstraat also lies at right angles to the pretty, tree-lined canal that links Bruges with Damme and, ultimately, Sluis, a tiny village over the border in Holland. The Sluis canal intersects with the wider and busier Leopoldkanaal just 2km to the northeast of Damme, and together they frame a delightfully scenic sliver of countryside dotted with whitewashed farmhouses and patterned by old causeways – perfect for cycling.

Arrival and information

There are several ways of reaching Damme, the most rewarding being the seven-kilometre cycle ride out along the tree-lined Bruges–Sluis canal, which begins at the Dampoort, on the northeast edge of the city centre. Cycle rental is available in Bruges (see p.156) and in Damme at Tijl en Nele, round the corner from the Stadhuis at Jacob van Maerlantstraat 2 (reservations advised; ☎050/35 71 92, ⊛www.tijlennele.be.tf; closed Wed; €10 per day).

You can also get from Bruges to Damme by canal boat, with excursions starting about 500m east of the Dampoort on the Noorweegse Kaai (Easter–Sept 5 daily each way; 40min; one-way €5, return €6.50); tickets are purchased on board. Connecting bus #4 from the Markt and the bus station runs to the Noorweegse Kaai to meet most departures – but check the connection with the bus driver before you set out.

Finally, you can reach Damme on city bus #799 from the bus station or the Markt (April–Sept 6 daily each way; 15min; one-way ticket €1.80, return €3.60). During the rest of the year, the bus runs less frequently and you'll be forced to hang around for longer than you'll want in Damme – if, indeed, you can make the return journey at all.

Damme has its own tourist office, across the street from the Stadhuis (mid-April to mid-Oct Mon–Fri 9am–noon & 2–6pm, Sat & Sun 10am–noon & 2–6pm; mid-Oct to mid-April Mon–Fri 9am–noon & 1–5pm, Sat & Sun 2–5pm; ☎050/28 86 10).

▲ BURG

The Stadhuis

Kerkstraat. No public access. Funded by a special tax on barrels of herrings, the fifteenth-century Stadhuis, just a few steps down Kerkstraat from the Sluis canal, is easily the best-looking building in the village, its elegant, symmetrical facade balanced by the graceful lines of its exterior stairway. In one of the niches you'll spy Charles the Bold offering a wedding ring to Margaret of York, who stands in the next niche along – appropriately, as the couple got spliced here in Damme,

a prestige event that attracted aristocratic bigwigs from all over western Europe.

St Janshospitaal

Kerkstraat. Easter–Sept Mon & Fri 2–6pm, Tues–Thurs, Sat & Sun 11am–noon & 2–6pm; €1.50. Just down the street from the Stadhuis, St Janshospitaal accommodates a small museum of five rooms and a dainty little chapel. Room 1 houses a couple of curiously crude parchment-and-straw peasants' pictures of St Peter and St Paul, while rooms 2 and 3 have some fine old furniture. Room 4, the main room, displays an enjoyable sample of Delftware and pewter, but it's the chimneypiece that grabs the attention, a Baroque extravagance with a cast-iron back-plate representing the penance of King David for the murder of Bathsheba's husband. Otherwise, the museum holds a mildly diverting assortment of liturgical objects, a potpourri of ceramic ware and folksy votive offerings.

Onze Lieve Vrouwekerk

Kerkstraat. May–Sept daily 10.30am–noon & 2.30–5.30pm; €1. From

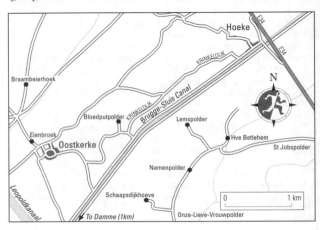

The Battle of Damme

In the summer of 1340, a French fleet assembled in the estuary of the Zwin to pre-pare for an invasion of England. To combat the threat the English king, Edward III, sailed across the Channel and attacked at dawn. Although they were outnumbered three to one, Edward's fleet won an extraordinary victory, his bowmen causing chaos by showering the French ships with arrows from a safe distance. A foretaste of the Battle of Crecy, there was so little left of the French force that no one dared tell King Philip of France, until finally the court jester took matters into his own hands: "Oh! The English cowards! They had not the courage to jump into the sea as our noble Frenchmen did." Philip's reply is not recorded.

St Janshospitaal, it's a couple of minutes' walk further down Kerkstraat to the Onze Lieve Vrouwekerk, a sturdy brick structure in classic Gothic style. The church is attached to a ruined segment of the original nave (open access) that speaks volumes about Damme's decline. The church was built in the thirteenth century, but when the population shrank it was just too big and so the inhabitants abandoned part of the nave and the remnants are now stuck between the present church and its clumpy tower. Climb the tower for panoramic views over the surrounding polders. The large and enigmatic, three-headed modern statue beside the tower is the work of the contemporary Belgian painter and sculptor Charles Delporte (born 1928).

Just beyond the church, on the right-hand side of Kerkstraat, a footpath branches off along a narrow canal to loop round the west side of Damme, an enjoyable ten–minute stroll through the poplars which brings you out just west of the village beside the Bruges–Sluis canal.

Cycling around Damme

Damme lies at the start of a pretty little parcel of land, a rural backwater crisscrossed by drowsy canals and causeways, each of which is shadowed by two long lines of slender trees which quiver and rustle in the prevailing westerly winds. This perfect cycling country extends as far as the E34 motorway, about 6km from Damme. There are lots of possible

▲ SIGNPOST IN COUNTRYSIDE NEAR DAMME

routes; if you want to explore the area in detail you should buy the appropriate Nationaal Geografisch Instituut map (1:25,000) in Bruges before you set out.

One especially delightful 15km round-trip takes in some of the area's most charming scenery. The route begins by leaving Damme to the northeast along the Brugge–Sluis canal, then crosses over the Leopoldkanaal and procedes to the hamlet of Hoeke. Here, just over the bridge, turn hard left for the narrow causeway – the Krinkeldijk – that wanders straight back in the direction of Damme, running to the north of the Brugge–Sluis canal. Just over 3km long, it drifts across a beguiling landscape before reaching an intersection where you turn left to regain the Brugge–Sluis waterway.

Shops

AHA
Kerkstraat 24. Mon noon–5pm, Tues–Sat 10am–5.30pm. Cosy little bookshop with a good section on tourist attractions in Bruges and its immediate surroundings.

Diogenes
Kerkstraat 22. Mon noon–5pm, Tues–Sat 10am–5.30pm. Pocket–sized bookshop focusing on literature and art, with many English titles.

Tante Marie Patisserie
Kerkstraat 38. Mon noon–5pm, Tues–Sat 10am–5.30pm. Smart, modern premises and the best cakes and pastries in town.

Cafés and restaurants

Bij Lamme Goedzak
Kerkstraat 13 ☎ 050/35 20 03. April–Sept daily except Thurs 11am–10pm; Oct–March Mon–Fri noon–2pm, Sat & Sun 11am–10pm. Arguably the best restaurant in Damme, this long-established place serves mouthwatering traditional Flemish dishes in the evening, often featuring wild game (mains around €20). It also sells its own house ales all day and has a garden terrace at the back and a pavement terrace at the front. Snacks and light meals are available at lunchtimes and in the afternoon.

Restaurant De Lieve
Jacob van Maerlantstraat 10 ☎ 050/35 66 30. Wed–Sun 6–10pm. Just behind the Stadhuis, this smart and formal restaurant offers the best of Flemish and French cuisine, with à la carte and set menus from €22.

▲ BIJ LAMME GOEDZAK

Ghent

Just twenty minutes by train from Bruges, the city of Ghent has a handsome set of medieval buildings, a lively restaurant scene and a bustling nightlife. Tourism is much less conspicuous here than in Bruges, and consequently Ghent feels like a much more authentically Flemish city. Like Bruges, Ghent prospered throughout the Middle Ages, but it also suffered from endemic disputes between the count and his nobles (who supported France) and the cloth-reliant citizens (to whom friendship with England was vital). Unlike Bruges, however, Ghent was rescued from economic decline after the demise of the cloth trade by an industrial boom that lasted for most of the nineteenth century. Ghent is still an industrial city, but in the last twenty years its ancient centre has benefited from an extraordinarily ambitious programme of restoration and refurbishment which has cleared away the accumulated grime.

The shape and structure of the city centre reflects Ghent's ancient class and linguistic divide. The streets to the south of the Korenmarkt (Corn Market), the traditional focus of the city, tend to be straight and wide, lined with elegant old mansions, the former habitations of the wealthier, French–speaking classes, while, to the north, Flemish Ghent is all narrow alleys and low brick houses. They meet at the somewhat confusing sequence of squares that spread east from the Korenmarkt to St Baafskathedraal, which is home to the fabulous Jan van Eyck altarpiece, *The Adoration of the Mystic Lamb*. Ghent's other leading attractions – principally the Gothic guild houses of the Graslei and the Castle of the Counts, Het Gravensteen – are within easy walking distance of

Arrival and information

There are four trains hourly from Bruges to Ghent; the return fare is €10. All these trains pull into Ghent's St Pieters train station, which is located about 2km to the south of the city centre. Trams run to the Korenmarkt, plumb in the centre, every few minutes from the covered tram stops beside St Pieters train station – check the destination sign at the front of the tram or ask the driver. The flat-rate fare per journey is €1; tickets can be bought from the driver.

Ghent's tourist office (daily: April–Oct 9.30am–6.30pm; Nov–March 9.30am–4.30pm; ☏09/266 52 32, ☏www.visitgent.be) is right in the centre of the city, in the crypt of the old cloth hall, the Lakenhalle. They have a wide range of city information, including a useful booklet detailing places of interest along with latest opening times. Note that although St Baafskathedraal – and the *Adoration of the Mystic Lamb* – can be visited every day, most of Ghent's other sights, including its museums, are closed on Mondays.

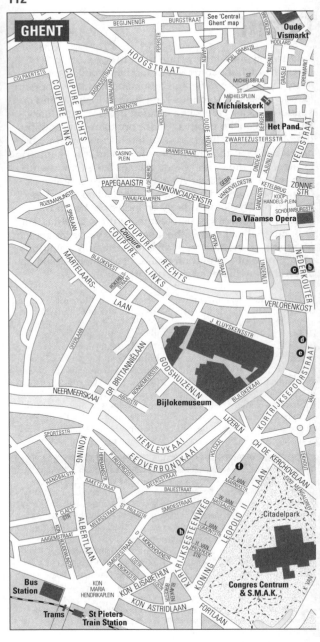

113

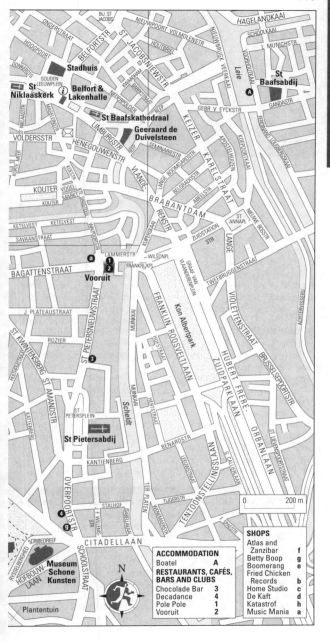

PLACES Ghent

ACCOMMODATION
Boatel   A
**RESTAURANTS, CAFÉS,
BARS AND CLUBS**
Chocolade Bar   3
Decadance   4
Pole Pole   1
Vooruit   2

SHOPS
Atlas and
  Zanzibar   f
Betty Boop   g
Boomerang   e
Fried Chicken
  Records   b
Home Studio   c
De Kaft   d
Katastrof   h
Music Mania   a

0   200 m

N

▲ ST BAAFSKATHEDRAAL, DETAIL OF BOSCH PAINTING

the Korenmarkt, the exception being the S.M.A.K. museum of contemporary art. It is, however, the general appearance of the city centre that appeals rather than any specific sight, its web of cobbled lanes and alleys overlooked by an enchanting medley of antique terraces and grand mansions, all woven round a tangle of canals.

St Baafskathedraal

St Baafsplein. Daily: April–Oct 8.30am–6pm; Nov–March 8.30am–5pm; free. The best place to start an exploration of the city is the mainly Gothic St Baafskathedraal (St Bavo's Cathedral), squeezed into the eastern corner of St Baafsplein. The third church to be built on this site, and 250 years in the making, the cathedral is a tad lopsided, but there's no

gainsaying the imposing beauty of its west tower with its long, elegant windows and perky corner turrets. Some 82m high, the tower was the last major part of the church to be completed, topped off in 1554 – just before the outbreak of the religious wars which were to wrack the country for the next one hundred years.

Inside the cathedral, the chapel displaying *The Adoration of the Mystic Lamb* (see opposite) is to the left at the beginning of the mighty fifteenth-century nave, whose tall, slender columns give the whole interior a cheerful sense of lightness, though the Baroque marble screen spoils the effect by darkening the choir. In the nave, the main item of interest is the rococo pulpit, a whopping, mid-eighteenth-century oak and marble affair, whose main timber of represents the Tree of Knowledge. Beyond, the walls of the south transept are covered with the hatchments of the Knights of the Golden Fleece (see p.75), who met here in 1445 and 1559, whilst

Boat trips and guided walking tours

Throughout the year, boat trips explore Ghent's inner waterways, departing from the Korenlei and Graslei quays, near the Korenmarkt (April–Oct daily 10am–6pm; Nov–March Sat & Sun 11am–4pm). Trips last forty minutes, cost €4.50, and leave roughly once every fifteen minutes, though the wait can be longer as boats often only leave when reasonably full.

Guided walking tours, organized by the tourist office, are particularly popular in Ghent. The standard tour comprises a two-hour jaunt round the city centre, including a 45-minute tour of the Stadhuis (April Sat & Sun at 2.30pm; May–Oct daily at 2.30pm; €6); advance booking – at least a couple of hours ahead of time – is strongly recommended.

the north transept displays a characteristically energetic painting by Rubens, *St Baaf entering the Abbey* of Ghent, dating from 1624.

Also in the transept is the entrance to the Romanesque crypt, which holds all sorts of religious bric-a-brac as well as a handful of early Flemish paintings moved here from the city's Museum voor Schone Kunsten (Fine Art Museum), which is closed for refurbishment until 2006. Amongst the paintings are two superb works by Hieronymus Bosch (1450–1516), the *Bearing of the Cross* and *St Jerome at Prayer*, plus Adriaen Isenbrandt's (d. 1551) *Rest during the Flight to Egypt*, a gentle painting showing Mary suckling Jesus, with a rural Flemish landscape as the backdrop.

The Adoration of the Mystic Lamb

Daily: April–Oct Mon–Sat 9.30am–4.45pm, Sun 1–4.30pm; Nov–March Mon–Sat 10.30am–3.45pm, Sun 1–3.30pm; €3. In a small side chapel to the left of the cathedral entrance is Ghent's greatest treasure, a winged altarpiece known as *The Adoration of the Mystic Lamb* (*De Aanbidding van het Lam Gods*), a seminal work of the early 1430s, though of dubious provenance. Since the discovery of a Latin verse on its frame in the nineteenth century, academics have been arguing about who actually painted the masterpiece. The inscription reads that Hubert van Eyck, "than whom none was greater", began the work, and Jan van Eyck, "second in art", completed it. However, as nothing else is known of Hubert, some art historians doubt his existence, arguing that Jan – who lived and worked in several cities, including Ghent – was entirely responsible for the painting, and claiming that only later, after Jan had firmly rooted himself in the rival city of Bruges, did the citizens of Ghent invent "Hubert" to counter his fame.

No one knows for sure, but what is certain is that in their manipulation of the technique of oil painting the artist – or artists – was able to capture a needle-sharp, luminous realism

PLACES Ghent

▲ CENTRAL GHENT SKYLINE

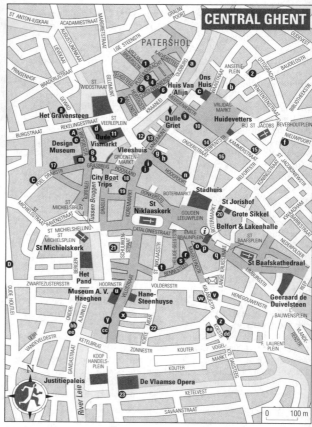

CENTRAL GHENT

that must have stunned their contemporaries. From the beginning, the altarpiece was famous across Europe. Philip II of Spain tried to acquire it; the emperor Joseph II disapproved of the painting so violently that he replaced the nude Adam and Eve with a clothed version in 1784 (exhibited today on a column just inside the church entrance); while near the end of World War II the Germans hid it in an Austrian salt mine, where it remained until American soldiers arrived in 1945.

The altarpiece is now displayed with its panels open, though originally these were kept closed and the painting only revealed on high days and holidays. Consequently, it's actually best to begin round the back with the cover screens, which hold a beautiful Annunciation scene with the archangel Gabriel's wings reaching up to the timbered ceiling of a Flemish house, the streets of a town visible through the windows. In a brilliant coup of lighting, the shadows of the angel dapple the room, emphasizing the reality of the apparition – a technique repeated on the opposite cover panel around the figure of Mary. Below, the donor and his wife, a certain Joos Vydt and Isabella Borlout, kneel piously alongside statues of the saints.

By design, the restrained exterior was but a foretaste of what lies within – a striking, visionary painting whose brilliant colours and precise draughtsmanship still takes the breath away. On the upper level sit God the Father (some say Christ Triumphant), the Virgin and John the Baptist in gleaming clarity; to the right

are musician-angels and a nude, pregnant Eve; and on the left is Adam plus a group of singing angels, who strain to read their music. The celebrated, sixteenth-century Flemish art critic Karel van Mander argued that the singers were so artfully painted that he could discern the different pitches of their voices – and, true or not, it is the detail that impresses, especially the richly embroidered trimmings on the cloaks. In the lower central panel the Lamb, the symbol of Christ's sacrifice, is depicted in a heavenly paradise – "the first evolved landscape in European painting", suggested Kenneth Clark – seen as a sort of idealized Low Countries. The Lamb stands on an altar whose rim is minutely inscribed with a quotation from the Gospel of St John, "Behold the Lamb of God, which taketh away the sins of the world". Four groups converge on the Lamb from the corners of the central panel. In the bottom right are a group of male saints and up above them are their female equivalents; the bottom left shows the patriarchs of the Old Testament and above them are an assortment of bishops, dressed in blue vestments and carrying palm branches.

On the side panels, approaching the Lamb across symbolically rough and stony ground, are more saintly figures. On the right-hand side are two groups, the first being St Anthony and his hermits, the second St Christopher, shown here as a giant with a band of pilgrims. On the left side panel come the horsemen, the inner group symbolizing the Warriors of Christ – including St George bearing a shield with a red cross – and the outer the

Just Judges, each of whom is dressed in fancy Flemish attire. The Just Judges panel is not, however, authentic. It was added during the German occupation of World War II to replace the original, which was stolen in 1934 and never recovered. The lost panel features in Albert Camus's novel *The Fall*, whose protagonist keeps it in a cupboard, declining to return it for a complex of reasons, one of which is "because those judges are on their way to meet the Lamb [but] there is no lamb or innocence any longer".

The Lakenhalle

St Baafsplein. Across from the cathedral, on the west side of St Baafsplein, lurks the Lakenhalle (Cloth Hall), a sturdy hunk of a building with an unhappy history. Work began on the hall in the early fifteenth century, but the cloth trade slumped before it was finished and it was only grudgingly completed in 1903. No one has ever quite

worked out what to do with the building, and today it's little more than an empty shell with the city's tourist office tucked away in the basement on the north side. This basement was long used as the town prison, whose entrance was round on the west side of the Lakenhalle through the Mammelokker (The Suckling), a grandiose Louis XIV-style portal that stands propped up against the main body of the building. Part gateway and part warder's lodging, the Mammelokker was added in 1741 and is adorned by a bas-relief sculpture illustrating the classical legend of Cimon, who the Romans condemned to death by starvation. He was saved by his daughter, Pero, who turned up daily to feed him from her breasts – hence the name.

The Belfort

St Baafsplein. Mid-March to mid-Nov daily 10am–12.30pm & 2–5.30pm; €3 (including optional guided tours, May–Sept daily at 2.10pm, 3.10pm & 4.10pm). Also on the west side of the Lakenhalle, just along from the Mammelokker, is the entrance to the adjoining Belfort (Belfry), a much-amended medieval edifice whose soaring spire is topped by a comically corpulent, gilded copper dragon. Once a watchtower-cum-storehouse for civic documents, the interior is now just an empty shell displaying a few old bells and statues alongside the rusting remains of a couple of old dragons, which formerly perched on top of the spire. The belfry is equipped with a glass-sided lift that climbs up to the roof, where consolation is provided in the form of excellent views over the city centre.

▲ THE BELFORT

The Stadhuis

Botermarkt. Guided tours only:
May–Oct Mon–Thurs daily at 2.30pm
(as the first 45min of the 2hr walking
tour organized by the tourist office;
see p.111); full 2hr tour €6, Stadhuis
only €3. Stretching along the
west side of the Botermarkt
is the striking and newly
restored Stadhuis (City Hall).
The buildling's main facade
comprises two distinct sections.
The later section, framing the
central stairway, dates from
the 1580s and offers a good
example of Italian Renaissance
architecture, its crisp symmetries
faced by a multitude of black-
painted columns. In stark
contrast are the wild, curling
patterns of the section to the
immediate north, carved in
Flamboyant Gothic style at the
turn of the sixteenth century to
a design by one of the era's most
celebrated architects, Rombout
Keldermans. The whole of the
Stadhuis was originally to have
been built by Keldermans, but
the money ran out when the
wool trade collapsed and the
city couldn't afford to finish it
off until much later – hence
today's discordant facade. Look
carefully at Keldermans' work
and you'll spot all sorts of
charming details, especially in
the elaborate tracery, decorated
with oak leaves and acorns as
well as vines laden with grapes.

Inside the Stadhuis, tours
gambol round a series of
halls and chambers, the most
interesting being the old Court
of Justice or Pacificatiezaal
(Pacification Hall), where the
Pacification of Ghent treaty
was signed in 1576. A plaque
commemorates this agreement,
which momentarily bound
the rebel armies of the Low
Countries (today's Belgium
and The Netherlands) together

▲ COAT OF ARMS, STADHUIS

against their rulers, the Spanish
Habsburgs. The carrot offered
by the dominant Protestants
was the promise of religious
freedom, but they failed to
deliver and much of the south
(present-day Belgium) soon
returned to the Spanish fold.
The hall's charcoal and cream
tiled floor is designed in the
form of a maze. No one's quite
certain why, but it's supposed
that more privileged felons (or
sinners) had to struggle round
the maze on their knees as a
substitute punishment for a
pilgrimage to Jerusalem – a
good deal if ever there was one.

St Niklaaskerk

Emile Braunplein. Mon 2–5pm, Tues–
Sun 10am–5pm; free. Back down
the slope from the Stadhuis, the
cobbled square to the west of
the Belfort is Emile Braunplein,
named after the reforming
burgomaster who cleared
many of the city's slums at the
beginning of the twentieth
century. The west edge of the
square abuts St Niklaaskerk,
an architectural hybrid dating
from the thirteenth century

▲ ST NIKLAASKERK

which was once the favourite church of the city's wealthier merchants. It's the shape and structure that pleases most, especially the arching buttresses and pencil-thin turrets which, in a classic example of the early Scheldt Gothic style, elegantly attenuate the lines of the nave. Inside, many of the original Baroque furnishings and fittings have been removed, thus returning the church to its early appearance, though unfortunately this does not apply to a clumsy and clichéd set of statues of the apostles. Much better is the giant-sized Baroque high altar with its mammoth representation of God glowering down its back, blowing the hot wind of the Last Judgement from his mouth and surrounded by a flock of cherubic angels.

The Korenmarkt

St Niklaaskerk marks the southern end of the Korenmarkt (Corn Market), a long and wide cobbled area where the grain which once kept the city fed was traded after it was unloaded from the boats that anchored on the Graslei dock (see opposite). The one noteworthy building here is the former post office, whose combination of Gothic Revival and neo-Renaissance styles illustrates the eclecticism popular in Belgium at the beginning of the twentieth century. The carved heads encircling the building represent the rulers who came to the city for the Great Exhibition of 1913; among them, bizarrely, is a bust of Florence Nightingale. The interior has recently been turned into a shopping mall.

St Michielsbrug

Behind the post office, the neo-Gothic St Michielsbrug (St Michael's Bridge) offers fine views back over the towers and turrets that pierce the Ghent skyline – just as it was meant to: the bridge was built in 1913 to provide visitors to the Great Exhibition with a vantage point from which to admire the city centre. As such, it was one of several schemes dreamed up to enhance Ghent's medieval appearance, one of the others being the demolition

▲ GUILDEHUIS VAN DE METSELAARS ON CATALONIESTRAAT

▲ CARVING OF CARAVEL, GUILD HOUSE OF THE FREE BOATMEN

of the scrabbly buildings that had sprung up in the lee of the Lakenhalle. The bridge also overlooks the city's oldest harbour, the Tussen Bruggen (Between the Bridges), from whose quays – the Korenlei and the Graslei – boats leave for trips around the city's canals (see box on p.114).

The guild houses of the Graslei

Ghent's boatmen and grainweighers were crucial to the functioning of the medieval city, and they built a row of splendid guild houses along the Graslei, each gable decorated with an appropriate sign or symbol. At no. 14 stands the Gildehuis van de Vrije Schippers (Guild House of the Free Boatmen), whose badly weathered sandstone is decorated with scenes of boatmen weighing anchor, plus a delicate carving of a caravel – the type of Mediterranean sailing ship used by Columbus – above the door. Medieval Ghent had two boatmen guilds: the Free, who could discharge their cargoes within the city, and the Unfree, who could not. The

Unfree Boatmen were obliged to unload their goods into the vessels of the Free Boatmen at the edge of the city – an inefficient arrangement by any standard, though typical of the complex regulations governing the guilds.

Next door, at Graslei 12–13, the seventeenth-century Coorenmetershuis (Corn Measurers' House) was where city officials weighed and graded corn behind a facade graced by cartouches and garlands of fruit. Next to this, at no. 11, stands the quaint Tolhuisje, built to house the customs officers in 1698, while the adjacent limestone Spijker (Staple House), at no. 10, boasts a surly Romanesque facade dating from around 1200. It was here that the city stored its grain supply for over five hundred years until a fire gutted the interior. Close by, the dainty Coorenmetershuis, at no. 9, was the original home of the city's Corn Measurers until the construction of their second, larger premises at Graslei 12–13 (see above). Finally, the splendid Den Enghel, at no. 8, takes its name from the angel bearing a banner that decorates the facade; the building was originally the stonemasons' guild house, as evidenced by the effigies of the four Roman martyrs who were the guild's patron saints.

At the north end of Graslei, just beyond the Grasbrug (bridge), the canal forks with the River Leie on the right and the Lieve canal to the left.

The Groentenmarkt

Just north of the Graslei, on the far side of Hooiard street, is the Groentenmarkt (Vegetable Market), one of the city's prettier squares, a jumble of old buildings which house two especially distinctive shops: Tierenteyn, the mustard specialist (see p.135), and the Himschoot bakery (see p.133). The west side of the square is flanked by a long line of sooty stone gables which were once the walls of the Groot Vleeshuis (Great Butchers' Hall), a covered market in which meat was sold under the careful control of the city council. The gables date from the fifteenth century but are in poor condition; the interior is only of interest for its intricate wooden roof.

The Korenlei

From the north end of the Graslei, the Grasbrug bridge leads over to the Korenlei, which trips along the western side of the old city harbour. Unlike the Graslei opposite, none of the medieval buildings have survived here, and instead there's a series of expansive, high-gabled Neoclassical merchants' houses, mostly dating from the eighteenth century. It's the general ensemble that appeals rather than any particular building, but the Gildehuis van de Onvrije Schippers (Guild House of the Unfree Boatmen), at no. 7, does boast a fetching eighteenth-century facade decorated with whimsical dolphins and bewigged lions, all bulging eyes and rows of teeth.

St Michielskerk

Onderbergen. April–Sept Mon–Sat 2–5pm; free. At the south end of the Korenlei rises the bulky mass of St Michielskerk, a heavy-duty Gothic structure begun in the 1440s. The city's Protestants seem to have taken a particularly strong disliking to the place, ransacking it

▲ DESIGN MUSEUM

▲ HET GRAVENSTEEN

arts. The wide-ranging collection divides into two distinct sections. At the front, squeezed into what was once an eighteenth-century patrician's mansion, is an attractive sequence of period rooms, mostly illustrating the Baroque and the Rococo. The original dining room is especially fine, from its fancy painted ceiling and Chinese porcelain through to its elaborate wooden chandelier and the intricately carved elm panelling.

The second section, at the back of the mansion, comprises a gleamingly modern display area used both for temporary exhibitions and to showcase the museum's eclectic collection of applied arts, dating from 1880 to 1940. There are examples of the work of many leading designers, but the Art Nouveau material is perhaps the most visually arresting, especially the finely crafted furnishings of the Belgian Henry van der Velde (1863–1957).

Het Gravensteen

St Veerleplein. Daily: April–Sept 9am–6pm; Oct–March 9am–5pm; €6. At the top of Jan Breydelstraat, turn right and cross the bridge to reach Het Gravensteen, the castle of the counts of Flanders, which looks sinister enough to have been lifted from a Bosch painting. Its cold, dark walls and unyielding turrets were first raised in 1180 as much to intimidate the town's unruly citizens as to protect them and, considering the castle has been used for all sorts of purposes since then (it was even used as

twice – once in 1566 and again in 1579 – and the repairs were never quite finished, as witnessed by the forlorn and clumsily truncated tower. The interior is much more enticing, the broad sweep of the five-aisled nave punctuated by tall and slender columns that shoot up to the arching vaults of the roof. Most of the furnishings and fittings are Gothic Revival, pedestrian stuff enlivened by a scattering of sixteenth- and seventeenth-century paintings, the pick of which is a splendidly impassioned *Crucifixion* by Anthony van Dyck (1599–1641) in the north transept. Trained in Antwerp, where he worked in Rubens' workshop, van Dyck made extended visits to England and Italy in the 1620s, before returning to Antwerp in 1628. He stayed there for four years – during which time he painted this *Crucifixion* – before migrating to England to become portrait painter to Charles I and his court.

The Design Museum

Jan Breydelstraat 5. Tues–Sun 10am–6pm; €2.50. Doubling back from St Michielskerk, it's a short walk to the Design Museum, one of the city's more enjoyable museums, which focuses on Belgian decorative and applied a cotton mill), it has survived in remarkably good nick. The imposing gateway comprises a deep-arched, heavily fortified tunnel leading to the courtyard, which is framed by protective battlements complete with wooden flaps, ancient arrow slits and holes for boiling oil and water.

Overlooking the courtyard stand the castle's two main buildings: the keep is on the right, while to the left is the count's residence, riddled with narrow, interconnected staircases set within the thickness of the walls. A self-guided tour takes you through this labyrinth; highlights include the count's cavernous state rooms, a gruesome collection of instruments of torture, and a particularly dank, underground dungeon. It's also possible to walk along most of the castle's encircling wall, from where there are pleasing views over the city centre.

Huis van Alijn Museum

Kraanlei 65. Tues–Sat 11am–5pm, Sun 10am–5pm; €2.50. One of the city's more popular attractions, the Huis van Alijn is a folklore museum that occupies a series of exceptionally pretty little almshouses set around a central courtyard. Dating from the fourteenth century, the almshouses were built following a major scandal reminiscent of *Romeo and Juliet*. In 1354, two members of the Rijms family murdered three of the rival Alijns when they were at Mass in St Baafskathedraal. The immediate cause of the affray was that one of each clan were rivals for the same woman, but the dispute went deeper, reflecting the commercial animosity of two guilds, the

weavers and the fullers. The murderers fled for their lives and were condemned to death *in absentia*, but were eventually – eight years later – pardoned on condition that they paid for the construction of a set of almshouses, which was to be named after the victims. The result was the Huis van Alijn, which became a hospice for elderly women and then a workers' tenement until the city council snapped it up in the 1950s.

The museum is divided into two distinct sections and although the labelling is skimpy throughout, explanatory, multilingual cards placed in each section give a bit more background. The first sequence of rooms – on the left-hand side of the courtyard on the floor above the entry desk – are thematic, illustrating particular aspects of traditional Flemish society, from those connected with funerals and death through to religious beliefs and popular entertainment. Across the courtyard is the chapel, a pleasantly gaudy affair built in the 1540s and now decorated with folksy shrines and votive offerings. When they aren't out on loan, the chapel is also home to a pair of wooden "goliaths", a common feature of Belgian street processions and festivals. Next to the church is a string of period rooms depicting local life and work in the eighteenth and nineteenth centuries with a printer's, a joiner's, a cobbler's and so forth.

Along the Kraanlei

Pushing on along the Kraanlei from the museum, it's only a few paces more to two especially fine facades. First up, at no. 79, is De Zeven Werken

Jacob van Artevelde

One of the shrewdest of Ghent's medieval leaders, Jacob van Artevelde (1290–1345) was elected captain of all the guilds in 1337. Initially, he steered a delicate course during the interminable wars between France and England, keeping the city neutral – and the textile industry going – despite the machinations of both warring countries. Ultimately he was, however, forced to take sides, plumping for England. This proved his undoing: in a burst of Anglomania, Artevelde rashly suggested that a son of Edward III of England become the new Count of Flanders, an unpopular notion that prompted a mob to storm his house and hack him to death. Artevelde's demise fuelled further outbreaks of communal violence and, a few weeks later, the Vrijdagmarkt witnessed a riot between the fullers and the weavers that left 500 dead. This rumbling vendetta – one of several that plagued the city – was the backdrop to the creation of the Huis van Alijn (see opposite).

van Barmhartigheid (The Seven Works of Mercy), a building which takes its name from the miniature panels which decorate its front. The panels on the top level, from left to right, illustrate the mercies of visiting the sick, ministering to prisoners and burying the dead, whilst those below (again from left to right) show feeding the hungry, providing water for the thirsty, and clothing the naked. The seventh good work – giving shelter to the stranger – was provided inside the building, which was once an inn, so, perhaps rather too subtly, there's no decorative panel.

The adjacent Fluitspeler (The Flautist), the corner house at no. 81, dates from 1669 and is now occupied by the *De Hel* restaurant. The six bas-relief terracotta panels on this facade sport allegorical representations of the five senses plus a flying deer; above, on the cornice, are the figures of Faith, Hope and Charity.

The Patershol

Behind the Kraanlei are the lanes and alleys of the Patershol, a tight web of brick terraced houses dating from the seventeenth century. Once the heart of the Flemish working

▲ STATUE OF JACOB VAN ARTEVELDE

-class city, this thriving residential quarter had, by the 1970s, become a slum threatened with demolition. After much to-ing and fro-ing, the area was saved from the developers and a process of gentrification begun, the result being today's gaggle of good bars and smashing restaurants. The process is still under way – one of the stragglers being the ongoing refurbishment of the grand old Carmelite monastery on Vrouwebroersstraat – and the fringes of the Patershol remain a ragbag of decay and restoration, but few Belgian cities can boast a more agreeable drinking and eating district.

Dulle Griet and the Vrijdagmarkt

At the north end of Kraanlei, an antiquated little bridge leads over to Dulle Griet (Mad Meg), a lugubrious old cannon whose failure to fire provoked a bitter row between Ghent and the nearby town of Oudenaarde, where it was cast. In the 1570s, fearful of a Habsburg attack, Ghent purchased the cannon from Oudenaarde. As the region's most powerful siege gun, able to propel a 340-kilogram cannon ball several hundred metres, it seemed a good buy, but when Ghent's gunners tried it out the barrel cracked on first firing. The useless lump was then rolled to the edge of the Vrijdagmarkt, where it has stayed ever since. Much to the chagrin of Ghent's city council, their Oudenaarde neighbours simply refused to offer a refund.

From Dulle Griet, it's just a few steps along Meerseniersstraat to the Vrijdagmarkt, a wide, open square that was long the political centre of Ghent, the site of both public meetings and executions – and sometimes both at the same time. In the middle of the square stands a nineteenth-century statue of the guild leader Jacob van Artevelde (see box p.125), portrayed addressing the people in heroic style. Of the buildings flanking the Vrijdagmarkt, the most appealing is the former Gildehuis van de Huidevetters (Tanners' Guild House), at no. 37, a tall, Gothic structure whose pert dormer windows and stepped gables culminate in a dainty and distinctive corner turret – the Toreken. Also worth a second glance are the lime-green Lakenmetershuis (Cloth Measurers' House), at no. 25, whose long windows and double entrance stairs are a classic example of eighteenth-century architecture, and the old headquarters of the trade unions, the whopping Ons Huis (Our House), a sterling edifice built in eclectic style at the turn of the twentieth century.

Bij St Jacobs

Adjoining the Vrijdagmarkt is busy Bij St Jacobs, a sprawling square sprinkled with antique shops and set around a sulky medieval church. The totempole-like modern statue on the near west (Vrijdagmarkt) side of the square is dedicated to a nineteenth-century Ghent folk singer, a certain Karel Waeri. The singer perches on top of the column, while below are carved illustrations of his best-known songs. The square hosts the city's biggest and best flea market (*prondelmarkt*) on Fridays, Saturdays and Sundays from 8am to 1pm.

Hoogpoort

Facing the Stadhuis, on the corner of Botermarkt and Hoogpoort, the *St Jorishof* restaurant occupies one of the city's oldest buildings, its heavy-duty stonework dating from the middle of the fifteenth century. This was once the home of the Crossbowmen's Guild, and although the crossbow was a dead military duck by the time it was built, the guild was still a powerful political force – and remained so until the eighteenth century. It was here, in 1477, that Mary of Burgundy (see p.70–71) was pressured into signing the Great Privilege confirming the city's commercial freedoms. She was obviously not too offended, as later that year this was where she chose to receive the matrimonial ambassadors of the Holy Roman Emperor, Frederick III. Frederick was pressing the suit of his son, Maximilian, who Mary duly married, the end result being that Flanders became a Habsburg fiefdom.

Lining up along the Hoogpoort, beyond St Jorishof, are some of the oldest facades in Ghent, sturdy if sooty Gothic structures dating from the fifteenth century. The third house along – formerly a heavily protected aristocratic mansion called the Grote Sikkel – is now the home of a music school, but the blackened remains of an antique torch-snuffer remain fixed to the wall beside the grand double doors.

Geeraard de Duivelsteen

Reep. No admission. Southeast of St Baafskathedraal lies the forbidding Geeraard de Duivelsteen, a fortified palace of splendid Romanesque design built of grey limestone in the thirteenth century. The stronghold, bordered by what remains of its moat and equipped with austere corner turrets, takes its name from Geeraard Vilain, who earned the soubriquet "duivel" (devil) either for his acts of cruelty or, according to other sources, because of his swarthy features and black hair. Vilain was not the only noble to wall himself up within a castle – well into the fourteenth century, Ghent was dotted with fortified houses (*stenen*), such was the fear the privileged few had of the rebellious guildsmen. The

▲ GEERAARD DEDUIVELSTEEN

PLACES | Ghent

last noble moved out of the Duivelsteen in about 1350 and since then the building has been put to a bewildering range of uses – at various times it served as an arsenal, a prison, a madhouse and an orphanage.

Lieven Bauwensplein and the van Eyck monument

Just south of the Duivelsteen is Lieven Bauwensplein, a square that takes its name from – and has a statue of – the local entrepreneur who founded the city's machine-manufactured textile industry. Born in 1769, the son of a tanner, Bauwens was an intrepid soul, who posed as an ordinary textile worker in England to learn how its (much more technologically advanced) machinery worked. In the 1790s, he managed to smuggle a spinning jenny over to the continent and soon opened cotton mills in Ghent. It didn't, however, do Bauwens much good: he over-borrowed and when there was a downturn in demand, his factories went bust and he died in poverty.

From the square, it's a short stroll north up Limburgstraat to St Baafskathedraal. On the way, you'll pass a monument to the Eyck brothers, Hubert and Jan, the painter(s) of *The Adoration of the Mystic Lamb*. The monument is a somewhat stodgy affair, knocked up for the Great Exhibition of 1913, but it's an interesting piece of art propaganda, proclaiming Hubert as co-painter of the altarpiece, when this is very speculative (see p.115). Open on Hubert's knees is the Book of Revelations, which may or may not have given him artistic inspiration.

Veldstraat

Ghent's main shopping street, Veldstraat, leads south from the Korenmarkt, running parallel to the River Leie. By and large it's a very ordinary shopping strip, but the mansion at no. 55, the Hôtel d'Hane-Steenhuyse, is of interest as the one-time hideaway of the refugee king of France, Louis XVIII (see box opposite). The grand facade of Louis's bolthole, dating from 1768, has survived in good condition, its elaborate pediment sporting allegorical representations of Time and History, but at present there's no access to the expansive salons beyond.

Pushing on down Veldstraat, another couple of minutes' walk brings you to a matching pair of grand, nineteenth-century Neoclassical buildings. On the left-hand side is the Justitiepaleis (Palace of Justice), whose pediment sports a large frieze with the figure of Justice in the middle, the accused to one side and the condemned on the other. Opposite stands the recently restored opera house – home of the Vlaamse Opera – whose facade is awash with carved stone panels.

▲ PALACE OF JUSTICE

Louis XVIII in Ghent

Abandoning his throne, Louis XVIII had hot-footed it to Ghent soon after Napoleon landed in France after escaping from Elba. While others did his fighting for him, Louis waited around in Ghent gorging himself – his daily dinner lasted seven hours and the bloated exile was known to polish off a hundred oysters at a sitting. His fellow exile, the writer and politician François Chateaubriand, ignored the gluttony and cowardice, writing meekly that "The French alone know how to dine with method". Thanks to the Duke of Wellington's ministrations, Louis was persuaded to return to his kingdom and his entourage left for Paris on June 26, 1815, one week after the Battle of Waterloo.

S.M.A.K.

Citadelpark ⊛ www.smak.be.
Tues–Sun 10am–6pm; €5. On the northeastern periphery of the leafy Citadelpark – and opposite the Museum Voor Schone Kunsten (Fine Art Museum; closed until 2006) lies S.M.A.K., the Stedelijk Museum voor Actuele Kunst (Municipal Museum for Contemporary Art). Housed in one part of a sprawling 1940s building that previously served as the city's casino, S.M.A.K. is one of Belgium's most adventurous contemporary art galleries. The ground floor is given over to temporary displays of international standing, and recent exhibitions have displayed the works of John McCracken and Pascale Marthine Tayou. Upstairs is a regularly rotated selection of sculptures, paintings and installations distilled from the museum's wide-ranging permanent collection. S.M.A.K possesses examples of all the major artistic movements since World War II – everything from surrealism, the CoBrA group and pop art through to minimalism and conceptual art – as well as their forerunners, most notably René Magritte and Paul Delvaux.

Perennial favourites include the installations of the influential German Joseph Beuys (1921–86), who played a leading role in the European avant-garde art movement of the 1970s, and a characteristically unnerving painting by Francis Bacon (1909–92) entitled *A Figure Sitting*. There's usually a healthy selection on display of the work of the Belgian Marcel Broodthaers (1924–76), whose tongue-in-cheek pieces include *Tray of Broken Eggs* and the trademark *Red Mussels Casserole*.

St Pietersabdij

St Pietersplein. Just to the east of S.M.A.K., Overpoortstraat runs north through the heart of the city's student quarter, a gritty and grimy but vivacious district, jam-packed with late-

▲ S.M.A.K.

night bars and inexpensive cafés. Overpoortstraat finally emerges on St Pietersplein, a very wide and very long square flanked by the sprawling mass of St Pietersabdij (St Peter's Abbey). The abbey dates back to the earliest days of the city and was probably founded by St Amand in about 640. The Vikings razed the original buildings three centuries later, but it was rebuilt on a grand scale and became rich and powerful in equal measure. As a symbol of much that they hated, the Protestant iconoclasts destroyed the abbey in 1578 and the present complex – a real Baroque monstrosity incorporating two courtyard complexes – was erected in the seventeenth and eighteenth centuries. The last monks were ejected during the French occupation in 1796 and since then – as with many other ecclesiastical buildings in Belgium – no one's been able to figure out what to do with the building. Today, much of the complex serves as municipal offices, but visitors can pop into the domed church, which was modelled on St Peter's in Rome, though the interior is no more than a plodding Baroque. To the right of the church, part of the old monastic complex has been turned into an arts centre, the Kunsthal St Pietersabdij, which houses temporary exhibitions (April to mid-Nov Tues–Sun 10am–6pm; free, though some exhibitions charge an entrance fee). Several of the adjacent cellars, rooms and corridors can also be explored with "Alison", a multilingual audioguide geared up for teens and pre-teens (€7). There's precious little to actually see here, but youngsters seem to enjoy this miniature labyrinth.

Vooruit

St Pietersnieuwstraat 23 ☎09/267 28 28, ⓦwww.vooruit.be. Café: Mon–Thurs 11.30am–2am, Fri & Sat 11.30am–3am & Sun 4pm–2am. It's a brief stroll north from St Pietersplein to *Vooruit*, a café-cum-performing arts centre that is, to all intents and purposes, the cultural heart of the city (at least for the under-40s), offering a varied programme of rock and pop through to dance.

▲TRAIN STATION

Vooruit also occupies a splendid building, a twin-towered and turreted former Festival Hall that was built for Ghent's socialists in an eclectic rendition of Art Nouveau in 1914.

Shops

Aleppo 1
Oudburg 72. Mon–Sat 2–7pm. Designer secondhand clothes for men and women, including big names like Ralph Lauren and Armani. Specializes in (believe it or not) cowboy outfits, with an abundance of leather and denim. The first floor is dedicated to 1960s and 1970s retro gear.

▲ ALEPPO 1

Alternatief
Baudelostraat 15 ☎09/223 23 11. Mon–Sat 11am–6.30pm, Fri from 10.30am. Great range of good-quality secondhand clothes and paraphernalia, though at slightly higher than average prices. Take a moment to browse the shop at the back as well, where you'll find everything from old cars to the last in kitsch. There's another branch just a few minutes' walk away at Ottogracht 12a.

Atlas and Zanzibar
Kortrijksesteenweg 100 ☎09/220 87 99, Ⓦwww.atlaszanzibar.be. Mon–Fri 10am–1pm & 2–6.30pm, Sat 10am–1pm & 2–6pm. Specialist travel bookshop offering a comprehensive selection of Belgian hiking maps and many English guidebooks.

Atmosphère
Hoogpoort 3 ☎09/224 40 22, Ⓦwww.atmosphere-gent.be. Tues–Sat 10am–noon & 1–6pm. Specializing in fabrics and modern home decoration, this attractively laid-out shop is definitely worth a visit, if only to browse.

Bethsabis
Hoogpoort 5 ☎09/225 54 54. Mon–Fri 9.45am–noon & 12.45–6pm, Sat 9.45am–6pm. Bargain shoe shop offering big names at low prices – snap up a pair of Prada shoes, for example, at half the regular high-street price.

Markets

Ghent has a good line in open-air markets. There's a large and popular flea market (*prondelmarkt*) on Bij St Jacobs and adjoining Beverhoutplein (Fri–Sun 8am–1pm), plus a smaller and a more sedate crafts and arts market (*kunstmarkt*) on St-Veerleplein (March–Oct Sat & Sun 10am–6pm). There's also a daily flower market on the Kouter, a square just off Veldstraat on the south side of the centre (7am–1pm), fruit and vegetables on the Groentenmarkt (Mon–Fri 7am–1pm, Sat 7am–5pm); and a bird market (not for the squeamish) on the Vrijdagmarkt on Sundays (7am–1pm).

Betty Boop

Overpoortstraat 110 ☎09/222 05 76. Daily 11am–12.30pm & 1.30–7pm, Sat until 6pm; closed Wed am. All the best Belgian comics, both traditional and new, plus a selection from America and Manga from Japan.

Boomerang

Kortrijksepoortstraat 142 ☎09/225 37 07. Tues–Sat 2–6.15pm. One of the best and most stylish retro and secondhand clothing shops in the city, and also has a good selection of shoes for men and women.

Casa

Veldstraat 65 ☎09/225 86 72. Mon–Sat 9am–6.30pm. This reasonably priced Belgian chain store offers household goods of the latest design. Specializes in tableware, furniture and decorations.

Claudia Sträter

Kalandestraat 6 ☎09/233 78 40. Mon–Thurs 9.30am–6pm, Fri & Sat 9.30am–6.30pm. This Dutch designer has gained an international reputation amongst women in the last few years and is especially popular in Belgium. The shop's light and spacious interior offers the perfect setting for Sträter's stylish collections, which include feminine tailored jackets and quality sporty casuals.

Coffee Roasters Sao Paulo

Koestraat 24 ☎09/225 44 11. Mon 12.30–6.30pm, Tues–Sat 9am–6.30pm. Excellent range of coffee, either pre-packed or freshly ground to your specifications, plus all sorts of other coffee paraphernalia.

Cora Kemperman

Mageleinstraat 38 ☎09/233 77 83, ⓦwww.corakemperman.nl. Mon–Sat 10am–6pm. This Dutch designer is gaining popularity amongst Belgian women for her unique but accessible designs in natural colours and fabrics.

Count's Gallery

Rekelingestraat 1 ☎09/225 31 27. Tues–Sun 10am–6pm. This odd little shop, just opposite the castle, sells an eclectic range of souvenirs, miniature models, postcards and so forth – great for kitsch gifts.

Dulce

Jan Breydelstraat 1 ☎09/223 48 73. Tues–Sat 10am–6pm. One of the best independent chocolate makers in Ghent – the handmade pralines are delectable. Prices start at €7 for a 250-gram box.

The English Bookshop

Ajuinlei 15 ☎09/223 02 36. Mon–Sat 10am–6pm. Small, but well-stocked secondhand bookstore selling all sorts of cheap English-language books, particularly on historical and military subjects.

The Fallen Angels

Jan Breydelstraat 29–31 ☎09/223 94 15, ⓦwww.the-fallen-angels.com. Wed–Sat 1–6pm. Mother and daughter run these two adjacent shops, selling all manner of old bric-a-brac from postcards and posters through to teddy bears and toys. Intriguing at best, twee at worst, but a useful source of unusual gifts.

FNAC

Veldstraat 88 ☎09/223 40 80, ⓦwww.fnac.be. Mon–Fri 10am–6.25pm, Sat 10am–6.55pm. Several floors of music, books and newspapers, including a good English-language section. It's also excellent for maps, including a comprehensive range of Belgian hiking maps, and sells tickets for most mainstream cultural events.

Fried Chicken Records

Nederkouter 47 ☎09/223 16 27. Mon–Fri 11am–7pm, Sat 11am–6pm. Founded by a top Ghent DJ, this shop is a cave of vinyl, the house speciality being drum 'n' bass.

Galerie St John

Bij St Jacobs 15 ☎09/225 82 62. Mon–Fri 2–6pm, Sat & Sun 10am–noon. One of several antique shops in the vicinity, this place sells an alluring range of *objets d'art* from silverware and chandeliers through to oil paintings. Great location, too – in an old church overlooking this busy square.

Grusenmeyer Interieur

Ajuinlei 27 ☎09/330 40 53, ⓦwww .grusenmeyer.be. Daily except Wed & Sun 11am–6pm. Run by a well-known city antiques family – and something of a local institution – this shop offers a wide-ranging selection of Asian antiques from Chinese furniture to Malayan porcelain and Cambodian bronzes.

Himschoot

Groetenmarkt 1 ☎09/225 74 05. Mon–Sat 7am–6.30pm, Sun 8am–5pm. This traditional, family-run bakery right in the centre of town has a real old-time feel and shelves heaped with all sorts of irresistible bread, as well as buns, fruit buns (*gebakjes met rozijnen*) and savouries. Don't be surprised if you have to queue.

Home Studio

Nederkouter 30 ☎0473 93 05 72 Wed, Fri & Sat 10am–6pm. Specialists in chic Italian contemporary furniture. Very minimalist, and all in neutral tones.

INNO

Veldstraat 86 ☎09/225 58 65. Mon–Thurs & Sat 9.30am–6pm, Fri 9.30am–7pm. This large Belgian department store specializes in clothes, and also has a good games and toys department, plus household goods.

Interphilia

St Baafsplein 4 ☎09/225 46 80. Mon–Sat 9.30am–5.30pm. Temptingly old-fashioned stamp shop (with a sideline in coins), with every nook and cranny stuffed to the gills.

Kaas Mekka

Koestraat 9 ☎09/225 83 66. Tues–Sat 8am–6.30pm. Literally the "Cheese Mecca", this small specialist cheese shop offers a remarkable range of traditional and exotic cheese – try some of the delicious Ghent goats' cheese (*geitenkaas*).

De Kaft

Kortrijksepoortstraat 44 ☎09/329 64 38, ⓦwww.dekaft.be. Daily 10am–

▲ THE FALLEN ANGELS

6pm. New and used books, some English-language, and CDs alongside lots of secondhand vinyl. Also has an English secondhand fiction section.

Katastrof

Kortrijksesteenweg 184 ☎09/220 60 76. Mon–Sat 9.30am–6.30pm. Rail upon rail of good-quality secondhand babywear and children's clothes at reasonable prices. Labels include Benetton, Timberland and Petit.

Kloskanthuis

Jan Breydelstraat 2 ☎09/223 60 93. Tues–Sat 10am–6pm. Ghent's one and only specialist lace shop, though the lace is actually part of a wider line in home linen. Well presented and displayed, though Bruges has far more lace shops – see p.104 for the best.

Mosaic@home

Hoogpoort 39 09/329 45 23, ⓦwww.mozaiek-workshop.be. Wed–Sat 11am–6pm. From Moroccan tables to Italian art, this is the place for all you'll ever need in the way of mosaics; they even run evening workshops if you fancy trying to make one yourself.

Music Mania

Bagattenstraat 197 ☎09/225 68 15, ⓦwww.musicmaniarecords.com. Mon–Fri 11am–6.30pm, Sat 11am–6.30pm. Four floors of CDs covering pretty much every genre (apart from classical and pop), from the latest releases to harder-to-find back-catalogue numbers.

Neuhaus

St Baafsplein 20 ☎09/223 43 74, ⓦwww.neuhaus.be. Daily 10am–6pm. Belgium's best chocolate chain,

with mouthwatering chocolate at around €10 for 250g – try their Manons, stuffed white chocolates, which come with fresh cream, vanilla and coffee fillings.

Obius

Meerseniersstraat 12 ☎09/223 82 69, ⓦwww.obius.be. Mon 1.30–6.30pm, Tues–Sat 10.30am–6.30pm. This friendly shoe and clothes shop has all the designer gear you need, including Prada, Miu-Miu and Patrick Cox, among many others.

Olivade

Koestraat 25 ☎09/225 40 42. Tues–Sat 10am–6pm. Gift shop-cum-foodstore specializing in all things to do with olives, from the stuffed variety (free tastings available) to oils, vinegar and marinades. Also has a small selection of takeaway pasta and rolls.

Olivier Strelli

Kalandestraat 19 ☎09/233 62 85, ⓦwww.strelli.be. Mon–Fri 9.30am–6pm, Sat 9.30am–6.30pm. The Ghent emporium of Olivier Strelli, arguably Belgium's leading designer, offering simple but stylish modern clothes for men and women, and specializing in smart tailored suits and zesty coloured fabrics. Expensive.

Oona

Bennesteeg 12 ☎09/224 21 13. Mon 2–6pm, Tues–Fri 11am–1pm & 2–6pm, Sat 11am–6.30pm. This minimalist shop stocks some truly individual creations, including Prada, Bikkembergs and Patrick Cox. Inevitably, the exclusiveness is reflected in the prices.

Peeters Delicatessen

Hoornstraat 9 ☎09/225 69 68.
Mon–Sat 9am–6.30pm. Petite
specialist cheese and wine shop
with a traditional feel to it, even
down to the owner's apron and
hat. Stocks an excellent range
of Belgian cheeses, as well as
a good selection of jam and
marmalade.

Tierenteyn

Groetenmarkt 3. Mon–Sat 8.30am–
6pm. This traditional shop, one
of the city's most delightful,
makes its own mustards,
wonderful, tongue-tickling stuff
that is displayed in shelf upon
shelf of ceramic jars. A small jar
will set you back about €6.

United Brands

St Niklaasstraat 2 ☎09/223 42
50, ⊛www.unitedbrands.be.
Mon–Sat 10am–6pm. Clothing
and equipment for all sports,
from tennis to skiing and
snowboarding. Stocks most
brands including Billabong,
Banana Moon and Quiksilver,
as well as all the usual large
sports names.

't Vlaams Wandtapijt

St Baafsplein 6 ☎09/223 16 43.
Mon–Sat 10am–6pm. The great
days of Belgian tapestry
manufacture are long gone,
but the industry survives,
albeit in diminished form,
and this shop features its
products. The large tapestries
on sale here are mostly
richly decorated modern
renditions of traditional
motifs and styles. As you
might expect, they're
expensive (from around
€500), though there's also a
good range of much more
affordable stuff like cushion
covers, handbags and other
smaller knick-knacks.

Cafés and restaurants

Amadeus

Plotersgracht 8 ☎09/225 13 85.
Mon–Sat 7–11pm, Sun noon–2.30pm
& 7–11pm. In the heart of the
Patershol, this busy, well-
established restaurant specializes
in spare ribs and has a relaxed
and convivial atmosphere, with
long tables, oodles of stained
glass, low ceilings and an
eccentric sprinkling of bygones.
Booking advised; mains around
€20.

Avalon

Geldmunt 32 ☎09/224 37 24. Café:
Mon–Sat noon–2pm; tearoom: Mon–Fri
2–6pm. This spick-and-span café
and tearoom offers a wide range
of well-prepared vegetarian
food, from salads to nut roasts,
served in a tranquil environment
and popular with the locals. The
daily lunchtime specials, at about
€8, are particularly popular.

PLACES

Ghent

▲ BIJ DEN WIJZEN EN DEN ZOT RESTAURANT

▲ *DE BLAUWE ZALM* RESTAURANT

Choose from one of the many different rooms or the terrace at the back in the summer.

Bij den wijzen en den zot

Hertogstraat 42 ☎ 09/223 42 30. Tues–Sat noon–2pm & 7–10pm. One of the best restaurants in the Patershol, serving up delicious Flemish cuisine with more than a dash of French flair – house specialities include eel, cooked in several different ways, and *waterzooi*. Soft lighting and classical music set the tone, and the premises are charming too – an old brick house of tiny rooms and narrow stairs with dining on two floors. Mains around €20.

Bistro 't Keteltje

Nederkouter 1 ☎ 09/233 22 55. Tues–Sat noon–2pm & 6–10pm; closed late Aug. Smart and neat little bistro with bright-white starched tablecloths and tasty daily specials from an international menu (mains around €18). It's adjacent to the Ketelvaart canal – though this is more an industrial eyesore than an attraction.

De Blauwe Zalm

Vrouwebroersstraat 2 ☎ 09/224 08 52. Mon & Sat 7–9.30pm, Tues–Fri noon–1.30pm & 7–9.30pm. Brilliant seafood restaurant – the best in town – serving up a superb range of seafood dishes ranging from cod, salmon, monkfish and haddock through to the likes of seawolf, turbot and John Dory. Fish tanks keep the crustacea alive and kicking, and the decor has a distinctly maritime feel – though it's all done in impeccable, ultra-cool style. Mains from €20. It's a very popular spot, so reservations are pretty much essential.

Brooderie

Jan Breydelstraat 8 ☎ 09/225 06 23. Tues–Sun 8am–6pm. Pleasant and informal café with a health-food slant, offering wholesome breakfasts, lunches, sandwiches and salads (from around €9), plus cakes and coffee. Also offers bed and breakfast (see p.150).

Budha Bar

Korte Meer 27 ☎ 09/223 23 32, ⓦ www.budhabar.be, Mon–Sat noon–2.30pm & 6–10.30pm. Concept food and lounge bar offering everything from tapas and dim sum through to pepper steak. Sit either up at the tapas bar and

▲ *BROODERIE* CAFÉ-RESTAURANT

choose dishes from the conveyor belt or order at one of the tables on the mezzanine floor. Downstairs is a lounge area complete with beanbags. Take-away also available.

Chocolade Bar

Sint Pietersnieuwstraat 99 ℡ 09/224 15 27, ⓦ www.chocoladebar.be. Mon–Thurs 10am–10pm, Fri & Sat 1–7pm. Chocolate aficionados will certainly get their fix in this bright and funky café devoted to the cocoa bean. Treats on offer range from the humble chocolate chip cookie to a chocolate fondue for two, as well as a plethora of chocolate-flavoured drinks, and coffee. Takeaway available.

De Hel

Kraanlei 81 ℡ 09/224 32 40. Mon & Thurs–Sun 6–10pm. This tiny, intimate restaurant in the Patershol, enhanced by candle-lit tables, Tiffany glass and classical music, offers delicious Franco-Belgian fare, with mains averaging €25. The building itself, dating from 1669, is adorned by charming terracotta reliefs of flying deer and the five senses topped off by representations of Faith, Hope and Charity.

Malatesta

Korenmarkt 35. Daily except Tues noon–2.30pm & 6–11pm. Informally fashionable café–restaurant decorated in strong, modern style and offering tasty pizza and pasta (from €12) at very affordable prices.

Marco Polo Trattoria

Serpentstraat 11 ℡ 09/225 04 20. Wed–Fri noon–2.30pm & 6–10pm, Sat & Sun 6–10pm; closed mid-Sept to mid-Oct. This simple rustic restaurant is part of the Italian "slow food" movement in which the emphasis is on organic, seasonal ingredients prepared in traditional style. The menu is small, but all the dishes are freshly prepared and delicious. Mains from €13.

't Marmietje

Drabstraat 30 ℡ 09/224 30 13. Tues–Sat noon–2.30pm & 6–10pm. Traditional family-run restaurant specializing in Flemish cuisine – a good place to try *Gentse waterzooi van kip* (chicken stew) and *Gentse stoverij* (stewed beef and offal cooked in dark beer). Now somewhat eclipsed by the newer and more fashionable restaurants of the Patershol, it's still a good bet and the prices are lower than most of its rivals. Daily specials around €10.

Pakhuis

Schuurkenstraat 4 ℡ 09/223 55 55, ⓦ www.pakhuis.be. Daily 11.30am–2.30pm & 7pm–midnight. Set in an intelligently remodelled old warehouse with acres of glass and metal, this lively bistro-brasserie is one of Ghent's more fashionable restaurants, attracting a wide-ranging clientele. The extensive menu features Flemish and French cuisine, with mains averaging €18. Bar area too.

Waterzooi

St Veerleplein 2 ℡ 09/225 05 63. Mon, Tues & Thurs–Sat noon–1.30pm & 7–9.30pm. Topnotch, split-level restaurant with pastel-painted walls, a wood-beamed ceiling, dappled lighting and stylish furniture. Mixed menu mostly in the French style offering the freshest of ingredients from beef and lamb through to lobster and monkfish, plus a good sideline in Flemish favourites, such as its namesake *waterzooi* (chicken or fish stew). Main courses weigh in at about €25.

Bars and clubs

Damberd Jazzcafe

Korenmarkt 19 ☎ 09/329 53 37, ⓦ www.damberd. be. Mon–Fri from 11am, Sat from 12pm, Sun from noon. This jazz café in the centre of Ghent offers a full programme of concerts, and is also a great venue just to meet, chat and have a few drinks while listening to some good music. Programmes change regularly – check the website for details.

▲ DULLE GRIET BAR

Decadance

Overpoortstraat 76 ☎ 09/329 00 54. Daily from 10pm until 8/10am, Sun until midnight. This funky club near the university (hence the abundance of students) offers one of the city's best nights out, with reggae, hip-hop, drum 'n' bass and garage-techno vibes.

't Dreupelkot

Groentenmarkt 12 ☎ 09/224 21 20. Daily: July & Aug 6pm until late; Sept–June 4pm until late. Cosy bar

▲ 'T DREUPELKOT BAR

specializing in *jenever*, of which it stocks more than 215 brands, all kept at icy temperatures – the vanilla flavour is particularly delicious. It's down a little alley leading off the Groentenmarkt.

Dulle Griet

Vrijdagmarkt 50. Daily noon–1am. Long, dark and atmospheric bar with all manner of incidental *objets d'art* and an especially wide range of beers.

Magazijn

Penitentenstraat 24 ☎ 09/234 07 08, ⓦ www.magazijn.be. Mon–Thurs noon–2pm & 6pm–1am, Fri 2–4pm & 6pm–4am, Sat & Sun 6pm–4am. Funky bar-cum-club showcasing everything from rock concerts and guest DJ nights to exhibitions of contemporary art, and also serves as a venue for the Ghent Festival. Serves inexpensive and filling bar food with lots of vegetarian options.

Pakhuis

Schuurkenstraat 4 ☎ 09/223 55 55, ⓦ www.pakhuis.be. Mon–Thurs 11.30am–1am, Fri & Sat 11.30am–2am. Set in a cleverly converted old warehouse and attractintg a young, friendly crowd, this is one of the best spots in town for a good night out. Try out the restaurant (see p.137), or just head down to the bar, where they do a good line in cocktails.

Pink Flamingo's

Onderstraat 55 ☎09/233 47 18, ⓦwww.pinkflamingos.be. Mon–Wed noon–midnight, Thurs & Fri noon–3am, Sat 2pm–3am, Sun 2pm–midnight. Weird and wonderful place – the interior is the height of kitsch, with plastic statues of film stars, tacky religious icons and Barbie dolls – if it's cheesy, it's somewhere in the decor. Attracts a groovy crowd, and is a great place for an aperitif or cocktails.

Pole Pole

Lammerstraat 8 ☎09/233 21 73, ⓦwww.polepole.be. Daily from 7pm until late. This place has a good cocktail menu, a world music (especially African) soundtrack, and dancing too. Adjoining it at no. 10 is the *Gringo Bar*, a Mexican-themed place that does much of the same thing.

Rococo

Corduwaniersstraat 57. Daily from 9pm until late. This intimate café–cum–

▲ DE TAP EN DE TEPEL BAR

bar attracts a diverse but cool clientele and is a perfect place to be on a cold winter evening, with candles flickering and the fire roaring. Stocks a good range of wines and beers, and also has home-made cakes.

De Tap en de Tepel

Gewad 7. Wed–Sat 6pm until late; closed most of Aug. This charming candle-lit bar (the name translates as "The Tap and Nipple") has an open fire and a clutter of antique furnishings. Wine is the main deal here, served with a good selection of cheeses.

De Tempelier

Meerseniersstraat 9. Mon–Sat 11am until late. Few tourists venture into this small, dark and intriguing old bar, which offers a vast range of beers at lower-than-usual prices, along with sometimes eccentric clientele and occasional live bands.

De Trollekelder

Bij St Jacobs 17. Mon, Wed & Thurs 6pm–1.30am, Fri 4pm–2.30am. This dark and atmospheric bar

▲ PINK FLAMINGO'S BAR

offers a huge selection of beers in an ancient merchant's house – don't be deterred by the trolls stuck in the window.

Den Turk

Botermarkt 3. Daily from 11am until late; closed during the Ghent festival. The oldest bar in the city, this tiny rabbit-warren of a place offers a good range of beers and whiskies and a famous plate of cheese with Ghent mustard. There's also frequent live music, mainly jazz and blues, and a great, if slightly highbrow, atmosphere. The beer menu is particularly good on Trappist brews.

Vooruit

St Pietersnieuwstraat 23 ☎ 09/267 28 28, ⓦ www.vooruit.be. Café-bar: Mon–Thurs 11.30am–2am, Fri & Sat 11.30am–3am, Sun 4pm–2am. In a splendid old building, dating from 1914, the Vooruit performing arts centre has good claim to be the cultural centre of the city (at least for the under-40s), offering a wide-ranging programme of rock and pop through to dance. The café-bar is a large barnlike affair that gets jam-packed till well into the morning.

Het Waterhuis aan de Bierkant

Groentenmarkt 9. Daily 11am until late. More than a hundred types of beer are available in this engaging, canal-side bar, which is popular with tourists and locals alike. Be sure to try Stropken (literally "noose"), a delicious local brew named after the time in 1453 when Philip the Good compelled the rebellious city burghers to parade outside the town gate with ropes around their necks.

▲ *DEN TURK BAR*

Accommodation

Accommodation

Bruges has over one hundred hotels, dozens of bed-and-breakfasts and several unofficial youth hostels, but vacancies still get tight at the height of summer, when you are well advised to book ahead or, at a pinch, ensure you get here in the morning before all the rooms have gone. Given the crush, many visitors use the hotel and B&B **accommodation service** provided by the city's tourist offices (see box on p.146) – it's efficient and can save you endless hassle. At other times of the year, things are usually much less pressing, though it's still a good idea to reserve ahead, especially if you're picky – it's easy enough, as almost everyone in the accommodation business speaks (at least some) English. Thirty-odd Bruges establishments are described below, but the city's tourist office issues an accommodation booklet providing comprehensive listings.

Fortunately, there's no need to stay on the peripheries of Bruges as the centre is liberally sprinkled with **hotels**, many of which occupy quaint and/or elegant old buildings. Standards are generally very high, though some places offer rooms of widely divergent size and com-

fort, and their worst (and not always cheapest) rooms can be distinctly small and cramped. The city's hoteliers are also wont to deck out their foyers in grand style, but this does not necessarily mean the guest rooms beyond are of a similar standard. Double rooms begin at about €60 per night, but you can pay over €300. Watch out for summer discounts and weekend specials, which can reduce costs by up to 35 percent.

B&Bs are generously distributed across the city centre too, and many offer an excellent standard of en-suite accommodation. Prices average €45–60 per double, rising to around €90 in some of the more luxurious establishments. Bruges has a handful of unofficial **youth hostels**, offering dormitory beds at around €13 per person per night. Most of these places, as well as the official HI youth hostel, which is hidden away in the suburbs, also have a limited supply of smaller rooms, with doubles at about €40 per night.

Hotels (over €80)

Adornes St Annarei 26 ☎050/34 13 36, ⊛www.adornes.be. Excellent three-star hotel in a* tastefully converted old

---

Hotel stars and prices

All licensed Belgian hotels carry a blue permit shield which indicates the number of **stars** allocated (up to a maximum of five). This classification system is, by necessity, measured against easily identifiable criteria – toilets, room service, lifts, and so on – rather than aesthetics or specific location, and consequently can only provide a general guide to quality and prices. Almost all hotels offer breakfast at no extra (or minimal) charge, ranging from a roll and coffee at the less expensive places through to full-scale banquets at the top end of the range. Finally, please note that the hotel room prices given below do not take into account special or weekend discounts.

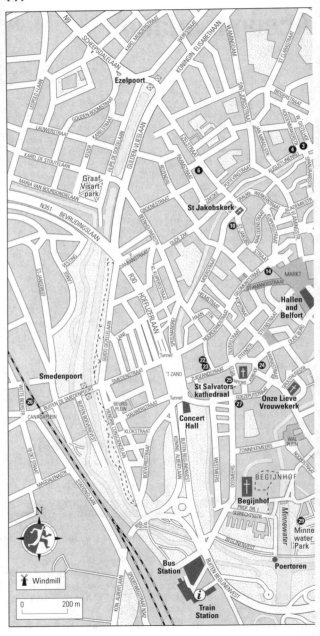

N

Windmill

0   200 m

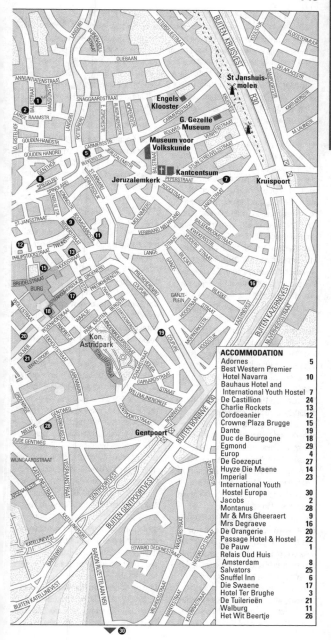

ACCOMMODATION

Adornes	5
Best Western Premier Hotel Navarra	10
Bauhaus Hotel and International Youth Hostel	7
De Castillion	24
Charlie Rockets	13
Cordoeanier	12
Crowne Plaza Brugge	15
Dante	19
Duc de Bourgogne	18
Egmond	29
Europ	4
De Goezeput	27
Huyze Die Maene	14
Imperial	23
International Youth Hostel Europa	30
Jacobs	2
Montanus	28
Mr & Mrs Gheeraert	9
Mrs Degraeve	16
De Orangerie	20
Passage Hotel & Hostel	22
De Pauw	1
Relais Oud Huis Amsterdam	8
Salvators	25
Snuffel Inn	6
Die Swaene	17
Hotel Ter Brughe	3
De Tuilerieën	21
Walburg	11
Het Wit Beertje	26

The tourist office accommodation service

Both of Bruges' tourist offices will make hotel and B&B reservations on your behalf at no charge, though they do require a small deposit, which is deducted from the final bill. There's one office inside the train station (April–Sept Tues–Sat 10am–1pm & 2–6pm; Oct–March Tues–Sat 9.30am–12.30pm & 1–5pm; ☎050/44 86 86), while the main office is bang in the centre at Burg 11 (April–Sept Mon–Fri 9.30am–6.30pm, Sat & Sun 9.30am–12.30pm & 2–6.30pm; Oct–March Mon–Fri 9.30am–5pm, Sat & Sun 9.30am–1pm & 2–5.30pm; ☎050/44 86 86, ☻www.brugge.be).

Flemish town house, with a plain, high-gabled facade – both the public areas and the comfortable bedrooms are decorated in bright whites and creams, which emphasize the antique charm of the place. It's in a great location, at the junction of two canals near the east end of Spiegelrei, and is very child-friendly. Delicious breakfasts. Doubles from €95.

Best Western Premier Hotel Navarra
St Jakobsstraat 41 ☎050/34 05 61, ☻www.hotelnavarra.com. This polished four-star occupies a grand Georgian mansion with a delightful wrought-iron staircase of craning swans and high-ceilinged public rooms. There are almost ninety bedrooms, decorated in brisk modern style, plus a pool, sauna and fitness area. It's set back from the road, behind its own courtyard, and just a short walk from the Markt. Part of the Best Western hotel chain. Doubles from €147.

De Castillion Heilige-Geeststraat 1
☎050/34 30 01, ☻www.castillion. be. Neat four-star hotel across from the cathedral set in two old converted Flemish houses with high crow-stepped gables – though the public areas are done out in a slightly overpowering repro antique style. Just twenty small but comfortable bedrooms with spruce and modern furnishings. Doubles €80 to €250.

Crowne Plaza Brugge Burg 10 ☎050/44 68 44, ☻www.crowneplaza.com. This prestigious four-star hotel, overlooking the Burg, occupies a good-looking modern building whose architectural features are designed to blend in with its historic surroundings. Boasts every facility, but then that's hardly surprising when the top-whack for a double room is a staggering €450. The cheapest rooms weigh in at about €125.

Dante Coupure 30 ☎050/34 01 94, ☻www.hoteldante.be. Clean and modern three-star built in traditional style with dormer windows and so forth – it's a little off the beaten track, but none the worse for that, and still within ten minutes' walk of the Markt. The 22 rooms are reasonably large, with crisp patterned furnishings, lots of wicker chairs and decor that errs precariously on the edge of blandness. The hotel overlooks one of the city centre's wider canals, an attractive stretch of water still used by heavy-laden barges. Doubles from €140.

Die Swaene Steenhouwersdijk 1 ☎050/34 27 98, ☻www.dieswaene-hotel.com. One of the most enjoyable hotels in Bruges. The unassuming brick exterior of this long-established, family-run four-star is deceptive, as each of the large rooms beyond is luxuriously furnished in an individual antique style, while the new annexe across the canal has ten sumptuously decorated "Pergola" suites complete with marble bathooms and lavish soft furnishings. The location is perfect too, beside a particularly pretty and peaceful section of canal a short walk from the Burg – which partly accounts for its reputation as one of the city's most "romantic" hotels. The hotel restaurant *Storie*, named after José Storie, the portrait artist who once lived in the antique attic apartment here, offers fine dining, and there's also a heated pool and sauna room. Breakfast is €15 extra, but will set you up for the best part of a day. Doubles from €185.

Duc de Bourgogne Huidenvettersplein 12 ☎050/33 20 38, ☻www.ducbourgogne.be. This three-star hotel's pride and joy is its restaurant-cum-breakfast room, overlooking a particularly picturesque slice of canal close to the Burg. The rest of the hotel is somewhat less appealing, however. The public rooms are in a heavy-duty neo-baronial style, while the ten guest rooms are furnished in a similar style and are a tad tired-looking – ask for one with a canal view. Best avoided in summer, when herds of tourists overwhelm the surrounding streets. Closed Jan and (usually) most of July. Doubles €180.

Egmond Minnewater 15 ☎050/34 14 45, ✆www.egmond.be. Set in an old manor house, this rambling three-star stands in a quiet location in its own gardens just metres from the Minnewater. The interior has wooden beamed ceilings and fine eighteenth-century chimneypieces, while the eight rooms are comfortable (if a little dour) and surprisingly affordable. Doubles from €135.

Europ Augustijnenrei 18 ☎050/33 79 75, ✆www.hoteleurop.com. Two-star hotel in a dignified late nineteenth-century town house overlooking a canal about five minutes' walk north of the Burg. It's a pleasant place to stay, even if the public areas are somewhat frumpy and the modern bedrooms are a little spartan. Doubles from €80.

Montanus Nieuwe Gentweg 78 ☎050/33 11 76, ✆www.montanus.be. Smart four-star hotel occupying a substantial seventeenth-century mansion kitted out in brisk modern style – although most of the rooms are at the back, in chalet-like accommodation at the far end of a large and attractive garden. There's also an especially appealing room in what amounts to a (cosy and luxurious) garden shed. Four star. Doubles from €108.

De Orangerie Kartuizerinnenstraat 10 ☎050/34 16 49, ✆www.hotelorangerie. com. Excellent four-star hotel in a surprisingly quiet location a couple of minutes south of the Burg. The original eighteenth-century mansion has been remodelled and extended in opulent style to house nineteen elegant bedrooms – though some are quite small – and there's a charming terrace bar at the back overlooking the canal. Usually closed for most of Jan. Doubles from €250.

Relais Oud Huis Amsterdam Spiegelrei 3 ☎050/34 18 10, ✆www.oha.be. Smooth, tastefully turned-out four-star hotel in a grand eighteenth-century mansion overlooking the Spiegelrei canal. Many of the furnishings and fittings are period, but more so in the public areas than in the (34) rooms. Doubles from €140.

Hotel Ter Brughe Oost-Gistelhof 2 ☎050/34 03 24, ✆www.hotelterbrughe. com. In an old and dignified merchant's house overlooking one of the prettiest canals in the city – and metres from the Augustijnenbrug bridge – this friendly, four-star hotel has 24 rooms. The cheaper rooms (€90), in the original part of the hotel, are rather tatty and outmoded, but the majority (€100–175) are well appointed and tastefully renovated, complete with bare wooden floors, oak beams and marble-finished bathrooms – though quite what the old English prints (of hunting, Queen Victoria, and so on) are doing on the walls is hard to fathom.

De Tuilerieën Dijver 7 ☎050/34 36 91, ✆www.hoteltuilerieen.com. Occupying an old and tastefully refurbished mansion close to the Burg, this delightful four-star is one of the best in town. Some of the 45 rooms overlook the Dijver canal, and breakfast is taken in a lovely neo-Baroque salon. Double rooms start at €300.

Walburg Boomgaardstraat 13 ☎050/34 94 14, ✆www.hotels-belgium.com. Engaging hotel in an elegant nineteenth-century mansion – with splendidly large doors – a short walk east of the Burg along Hoogstraat. The rooms are smart and comfortable, and there are also capacious suites. Doubles from €150.

Hotels (under €80)

Bauhaus Hotel Langestraat 133 ☎050/34 10 93, ✆www.bauhaus.be. Next to the *Bauhaus Hostel* (see p.149), this one-star hotel offers 21 very spartan rooms with shower and basin. Very popular with backpackers thanks to its cheap singles, doubles, triples and quads, but don't expect too much in the way of creature comforts, and the rooms are a little dingy. Laid-back, occasionally boisterous atmosphere plus a (usually) friendly clientele. Free parking available. Doubles €36.

Cordoeanier Cordoeaniersstraat 18 ☎050/33 90 51, ⊛www.cordoeanier.be. Medium-sized, family-run two-star handily located in a narrow side street a couple of minutes' walk north of the Burg. Mosquitoes can be a problem here, but the small rooms are clean and pleasant. Doubles from €75.

De Goezeput Goezeputstraat 29 ☎050/34 26 94, ℗050/34 20 13. Set in a charming location on a quiet street near the cathedral, this outstanding two-star hotel occupies an immaculately refurbished eighteenth-century convent complete with wooden beams and oodles of antiques. A snip, with en-suite doubles from €70.

Imperial Dweersstraat 24 ☎050/33 90 14, ℗050/34 43 06. Nothing out of the ordinary, but this old terrace house offers a handful of perfectly adequate en-suite rooms at a reasonable price – note that they are much more appealing than those in the annexe. A couple of doors down from the *Passage* hotel and hostel (see below and opposite). No credit cards. Two star. Doubles from €70.

Jacobs Baliestraat 1 ☎050/33 98 31, ⊛www.hoteljacobs.be. Pleasant three-star set in a creatively modernized old brick building complete with a precipitous crow-step gable – it's in a quiet location in an attractive part of the centre a ten-minute walk to the northeast of the Markt. The 23 rooms are decorated in brisk modern style, though some are really rather small. Doubles from €70.

Passage Hotel Dweersstraat 28 ☎050/34 02 32, ⊛www.passagebruges. com. A ten-minute stroll west of the Markt, this place is a real steal, with simple but well-maintained en-suite doubles for just €60, plus doubles with shared facilities from €40 and three-bed (€45) and four-bed (€60) rooms. It's a very popular spot and there are only ten rooms (four en suite), so advance reservations are pretty much essential. The busy bar serves inexpensive meals and is a favourite with backpackers.

De Pauw St Gilliskerkhof 8 ☎050/33 71 18, ⊛www.hoteldepauw.be. This competent – if not particularly exciting – two-star family-run establishment occupies an unas-

suming brick building in a pleasant, quiet part of town across from St Gilliskerk. Has eight sparse but perfectly adequate rooms, six en suite. Ask for the recently renovated room at the top, which is decidedly brighter than the others and overlooks the garden. Closed Jan. Doubles with shared facilities from €65; with en suite €75.

Salvators St-Salvatorskerkhof 17 ☎050/33 19 21, ⊛www.hotelsalvators. be. Pleasant hotel with bright, cosy rooms – ask for one with a Jacuzzi, fish tank or fireplace – housed in a handy location, metres from the cathedral. The bar downstairs has a large brick fireplace and comfortable sofas. Doubles from €70.

Bed and breakfast

Het Wit Beertje Witte Beerstraat 4 ☎050/45 08 88, ℮info@hetwitbeertje. Cosy little guesthouse-cum-B&B with three en-suite rooms, run by a friendly owner who has a fondness for bears. It's located just west of the city centre, off Canadaplein, beyond the Smedenpoort. No credit cards. Doubles from €50.

Huyze Die Maene Markt 17 ☎050/33 39 59, ⊛www.huyzediemaene.be. Excellent option above a brasserie plumb in the centre of town overlooking the Markt, with two cosy deluxe rooms and one spacious top-floor suite, each decorated in grand style. Closed Feb. Doubles €115.

Mr & Mrs Gheeraert Riddersstraat 9 ☎050/33 56 27, ℮paul.gheeraert@ skynet.be. The three en-suite guest rooms here are bright and smart, and occupy the top floor of a creatively modernized old house a short walk east from the Burg. No credit cards. Minimum two-night stay. Closed January. Doubles from €55.

Mrs Degraeve Kazernevest 32 ☎050/34 57 11, ⊛www.stardekk.com /bedbreakfast. Relaxed, friendly B&B with two eclectically decorated en-suite rooms, situated on the eastern edge of town; not far from the Kruispoort, which means that you miss the tourist droves – but then it's a fair old hike to the Markt. Mannequins and dolls abound, as well as a number of unusual features such as a musical toilet and the couple's very own bottled beer. Free pick-up from the train station. No credit cards. Doubles from €45.

Hostels

Bauhaus International Youth Hostel Langestraat 135 ℡050/34 10 93, ⓦwww.bauhaus.be. Laid-back hostel with few discernible rules, several large dormitories (sleeping up to eight people) and a mish-mash of double (€36) and triple rooms (€51), plus one single (€24). It's not for the fastidious, however: the place is far from neat and trim. There's bike rental, currency exchange and lockers, and the popular downstairs bar serves filling meals. The hostel is situated about fifteen minutes' walk east of the Burg, next to the bargain-basement *Bauhaus Hotel* (see p.147). From €11 per person for a dorm bed.

Charlie Rockets Hoogstraat 19 ℡050/33 06 60, ⓦwww.charlierockets.com. The rooms in this busy hostel may not be as pristine as they were when it opened five years ago, but it steals a march on its rivals by being so much closer to the Markt. Accommodation is either in dorms (sleeping four or six) or double rooms. It's above a busy American-style bar (see p.64), so light sleepers may prefer to go elsewhere. Plans are afoot to open a restaurant next door in early 2005. Dormitory beds from €14, or €17 with breakfast. Doubles €43, including breakfast.

International Youth Hostel Europa Baron Ruzettelaan 143 ℡050/35 26 79, ⓦwww.vjh.be. Big, modern HI-affiliated hostel in its own grounds, a (dreary) 2km south of the centre in the suburb of Assebroek. There are over two hundred beds in a mixture of rooms from singles through to six-bed dorms. Breakfast is included in the price. Lockout 10am–1pm, (until 5pm on Sunday); closed Christmas to mid-January. City bus #2 from the train station goes within 100m – ask the driver to let you off. Dorm beds €13.75 (non-HI members €16.75). Doubles €16.30/€20.50.

Passage Dweersstraat 26 ℡050/34 02 32, ⓦwww.passagebruges.com. The most agreeable hostel in Bruges, accommodating fifty people in ten comparatively comfortable dormitories (all with shared bathrooms). Located in an old and interesting part of town, about ten minutes' walk west of the Markt. Meals are available at the bar, and guests get a free beer with food. Rates from €12 for a dorm bed, €3 extra for breakfast.

Snuffel Inn Ezelstraat 47–49 ℡050/33 31 33, ⓦwww.snuffel.be. Well-run hostel to the west of the centre with four- to

Holiday apartments

There are plenty of holiday apartments in Bruges, available for both long- and short-term rental, and the best offer good value in attractive surroundings. The comprehensive accommodation brochure issued by the city's tourist office details over fifty of them, with prices ranging from as little as €350 per week for two people (€425 for four) up to around €450 (€600). The tourist office does not, however, arrange holiday apartment lettings – these must be arranged direct with the lessor. As ever, advance booking is strongly advised. One recommendation is the top-quality holiday apartment rented out by Mr and Mrs Dieltiens (℡050/33 42 94, ⓦwww.bedandbreakfastbruges.be). This apartment, in the Huyze de Blockfluyt, is centrally located, at Peerdenstraat 16, and comprises a two-storey flat that sleeps up to four people, with wooden floors, exposed beams and a kitchen; it also has an additional attic bed above the main double complete with its own dinky little ladder. Prices are from €420 per week for two. Alternatively, Mr & Mrs Gheeraert (see details of their B&B opposite) run an immaculate apartment and two studios in the Ridderspoor, a beautiful nineteenth-century house at Riddersstraat 18. The ground-floor studio has a private terrace, while the top-floor open-plan apartment offers a (limited) view of the Burg. Both have their own kitchen and there's a minimum three-night stay. Studio prices are from €490 per week for two.

twelve-bed dorms and a cosy, laid-back bar which stays open till late. Rooms and bathrooms have recently been decorated in lively contemporary style by local artists and art students. Bikes are available for rent, and there's live music every fortnight plus regular barbecues in summer. Dorm beds from €11; breakfast €3. Reservations recommended April–Sept.

Staying in Ghent

Ghent has several especially enticing places to stay and prices are slightly lower than in Bruges. The Ghent tourist office, in the centre of the city in the crypt of the old cloth hall, the Lakenhalle (daily: April–Oct 9.30am–6.30pm; Nov–March 9.30am–4.30pm; ☎09/266 52 32, ⊛www.visitgent.be), publishes a free and comprehensive brochure detailing local accommodation, including hotels and hostels along with prices, but not its B&Bs. They also operate a **hotel accommodation service** – especially useful in July and August, when vacant rooms are thin on the ground.

Boatel Voorhoutkaai 44 ☎09/267 10 30, ⊛www.theboatel.com. Arguably the most distinctive of Ghent's hotels, the two-star *Boatel* is, as its name implies, a converted boat – an imaginatively and immaculately refurbished canal barge, to be precise. The seven bedrooms are decked out in crisp, modern style – five standard at €95 and two deluxe at €119 – and breakfasts, taken on the deck, are first-rate. The boat is moored in one of the city's outer canals, a ten- to fifteen-minute walk east from the centre. Doubles from €95.

Brooderie Jan Breydelstraat 8 ☎09/225 06 23. Three neat and trim little rooms above an appealing little café, handily located in the city centre, near the Korenmarkt. B&B costs €60/65 for a double, €40 for a single. Breakfast is excellent.

Erasmus Poel 25 ☎09/224 21 95, ⊛ehotel.erasmus@proximedia.be. Another contender for Ghent's most distinctive hotel, this small family-run establishment is located in an old and commodious town house a few metres from the Korenlei. Each room is thoughtfully decorated – though it's a touch twee in places – and furnished with antiques. The breakfast is excellent and the family are very friendly. Reservations strongly advised in summer. Closed mid-Dec to mid-Jan. Doubles from €100.

Gravensteen Jan Breydelstraat 35 ☎09/225 11 50, ⊛www.gravensteen .be. Set in a great location, close to the castle, this very pleasant medium-sized three-star hotel occupies an attractively restored nineteenth-century mansion adorned with Second Empire trimmings. The rooms in the annexe and in one wing of the original building are smart and relatively spacious, with crisp and pleasing modern furnishings. Several of the older rooms are, however, poky beyond belief. Doubles from €125.

Monasterium Poortackere Oude Houtlei 56 ☎09/269 22 10, ⊛www .monasterium.be. This unusual one-star hotel-cum-guesthouse occupies a rambling and frugal former monastery dating from the nineteenth century. Guests have a choice between spick and spartan, en-suite rooms in the hotel section (€145) or the more authentic monastic-cell experience in the guesthouse, either en suite or with shared facilities (both €120). Breakfast is taken in the old chapterhouse.